I0453859

It Will Be Okay

JAMES OLDS

Copyright © 2023 by James Olds.

ISBN 979-8-88945-188-4 (softcover)
ISBN 979-8-88945-190-7 (hardcover)
ISBN 979-8-88945-189-1 (ebook)

All rights reserved. No part of this book may be reproduced or
transmitted in any form or by any means, electronic or mechanical,
including photocopying, recording, or by any information storage and
retrieval system without express written permission from the author,
except in the case of brief quotations embodied in critical reviews and
certain other noncommercial uses permitted by copyright law.

Printed in the United States of America.

Brilliant Books Literary
137 Forest Park Lane Thomasville
North Carolina 27360 USA

PREFACE

I have written several books in my life ranging from military manuals to an actual nonfictional novel. None of which, to me, are more important than this simple manuscript. Now I realize that in writing the use of the first-person is never quite acceptable. So, for this please excuse me because I have never written a manuscript along the level of an almost a sheer autobiography of the events that transpired in my life for the greater part of 2015-2018. The events that I reveal in this short little manuscript are true and presented in the best of my ability. I crafted this manuscript as I was directed to do, by the Holy Spirit as they occurred. These events have been life-changing for me, and I wish to share them with the world. My only true deviation from the truth is that the names of been changed to protect those that were intimately involved so that they do not gain any notoriety negative or positive. To lend some credence what I write, I have attempted to deliver this message this by painting it within the background of the clinical social worker interviewing a veteran, such as myself. I chose this background, to help tell the story as a more fluid content rather than just laying it out for all to see and read. Besides, any veteran with a spinal cord injury (SCI), such as myself, are required to see a social worker, at a minimum, once a year. Hopefully this chosen framework can help in conveying my transformation to becoming a Christian.

As such, I trust this given format will not deter from the overall message and testimony. There are many skeptics and naysayers believe in The Big Bang Theory or some other modem-day explanation for the creation of life. The same naysayers and skeptics are too willing to watch movies that depict evil spirits affecting the lives of average individuals, yet they are too quick to cast doubt on the truth about events. I just hope and pray that readers can overlook my excessive use of the first-person because this is the only way I know to express it. I further pray that the events that occurred to me here in some way help save at least one other person from suffering a true fate that I was destined for me before I became born-again. For those of us with faith, *it will be okay*.

CHAPTER ONE

Introduction

*A*s a social worker at a local Veterans Administration hospital, Catherine felt that she was dedicated to her work in helping veterans with whatever problems that seem to plague them. Some may call her a "late bloomer" considering she was in her late 50s and had just recently received her degree after putting three kids through school. Her own husband had walked out many years ago after numerous affairs and was even rumored to have fathered several other children outside of wedlock. However, her main interest was in the mental health of veterans which she contributed to her father who had come home from Vietnam as a very abusive man. She vaguely remembered him prior to his departure shortly after Christmas in 1967. She remembered him as being a happy person, always laughing and full of fun. When he returned home, however, he seemed to be changed and a rather broken individual. Drinking frequently was a misnomer, "*drinking continuously*" she thought to herself as she pulled the next patient file from her stack of new cases. She always like to review these new cases over a cigarette and a café latte out in the courtyard. "*Now let's see who we have today*" she thought to herself as she inhaled deeply on her cigarette. "*White male, 61 years old quadriplegic*" she began as she took a sip of her coffee. "*Says here that his wife tried to kill him*," intrigued by what she was reading she carefully placed her coffee down next to her and turned the page all the while thinking "*he probably deserved it*." Continuing on "*what would drive someone who had been married for over 25 years to this point*" she questioned to herself as she stamped out her remaining cigarette in the appropriate receptacle. Continuing to read the file while sipping on the remains of her coffee, she walked back towards the door to reenter the building, "*well this should be an interesting case*" she thought as she walked through the automatic doors.

"Hello," she began as she entered her office and greeted her patient that was already sitting there waiting for her. She reached out with a very stiff and un-easy and shake all the while thinking to herself "*I still have to master this.*" For her handshake was more robotic than an automatic gesture. "You must be John" she began. Just as soon as she offered her hand, she realized her folly and retracted it, "sorry" *I must read my case files more carefully*!

"Yes ma'am" John replied with a smile. Even though he had been out of the military for over 20 years this had become just his way of speaking to individuals, rather on the formal side. "No worries" he reassured her "most people are not quite sure how to greet me" he said again with a smile. "I guess you're here to tell me how messed up I am" he said with a smile. "I'm not really sure why this is necessary because I feel quite fine. I mean, I feel quite comfortable resting in the hands of my Lord."

"My, how convenient it must be for individuals such as this to speak of the Lord, all the while trying to hide what problems they may have" Catherine thought, and a wry smile came to her face. "Why don't you tell me a little about yourself, I mean in a nutshell why don't you describe what is going on in your life?" Catherine asked as she took her seat.

"What you mean" John asked as he manipulated the control mechanisms on his power chair to adjust himself slightly. "I am not really sure why I'm actually here; I mean I'm not even aware of why this appointment was even necessary."

"Well," she began, "it is customary within the VA system for the veteran to visit with the social worker at least once a year" she explained. "I generally like to start these sessions off with you describing your life" she said while reaching into her purse. After a brief moment she pulled out a small digital recorder and clicked it on, then placed it on her desk in front of her.

"Where does one begin to describe one's life?" John asked inquisitively to no one in particular but rather to one himself. John was a mere shadow of his former self. Confined to a power chair he was a quadriplegic unable to move anything from the neck down. As being confined to a power chair weight gain was almost inevitable as well as bladder infections that would end up putting him in the hospital for three or four days at a time. In just a few years John had gone from a 73-inch, 180 pounds near middle-aged athlete who, at one time, even sported a 32-inch waist caressed in leather pants. Despite the best advancements in Multiple Sclerosis (MS) research, nothing had stopped the relentless progression of the disease. It was no wonder that the condition itself would be too much for superficial individuals to endure. Often John would reflect on what his grandfather once said "one's character is not defined on a day-to-day basis when everything is going well. But rather one's character is defined when disaster strikes! It is then when one's character is defined and how they resolve the issue they are confronted with." John thought about this especially considering he revered his grandfather.

When asked of the disease, John often replied "it's like being placed in a woodchipper feet first. You get to see everything go before you realizing there's nothing you can do about it and realizing that are everything were just material will objects that didn't really matter much to anyone else." This reflected more of John's general outlook and personality rather than philosophical viewpoint. "So, how does one define one's life when you're just one bladder infection away from seeing the end?" This type of question can only be answered if one understands what the true purpose of life was to begin with. John did not lead a life of the great notoriety. He was not a magnificent artist or tremendous statesman. Nor did he live a life of tremendous pain and suffering, eking out an existence on the edge of society. If nothing else and despite John's own delusions of grandeur, John had resigned himself to understanding that he had led a rather typical, somewhat upper-middle-class life without much to show for it other than some material goods, a string of debts and about two coins to show for savings. But through it all, John actually found a closer relationship to God than he ever thought possible. Still not understanding the "big picture" as is often referred to, John actually resigned himself to being quite happy as long as he was able to live on the fringe of heaven, as long as he was there, everything was right with the world, as far as he was concerned.

"So how does one describe one's life?"

"John, John" said the social worker as she gently shook his shoulder to regain his attention. "John, are you going to answer my question" she said softly if only to gain his confidence. Readjusting herself in her chair and picking up her pad of paper and pencil off the nearby coffee table, Catherine leaned back in her chair and said again "how do you describe your life?" She liked taking notes on a pad of paper with a pencil, rather than some new-age electronic device. If for nothing else the pencil gave her a placebo when she was unable to smoke a cigarette at her leisure.

"Where does one begin to tell the story that defines his life?" John again started on the question while rubbing his chin against the joystick knob that was in front of him. "Originally" began John as he slowly adjusted his chair forward, John took a sip of water from a straw that was perched next to his cheek. There was a glass and a government issued office water pitcher sitting in front of him for such a purpose. But in this particular case these were quite useless. "*Funny*" he thought to himself quickly, as the water-built confidence that his speech would be unbroken, John took a small swallow of water that had remained in his mouth and began again. "I was originally married to my high school sweetheart in 1976." Adjusting, again, slightly in his seat, "it was near disaster from the beginning" John said with a wry smile. "You see, we were both very young. I was only 20 days out of high school, and she had dropped out at the beginning of 12th grade. Considering I was the only one working and she was at home she was to maintain the house." Turning his head slightly so as to face Catherine more directly, John said, "this she did not do very well" while shaking his head in agreement. "You might say she was downright poor at doing any household chores. So poor were the house conditions that we would fight on a regular basis." Raising his voice in a sign of desperation. "To make matters worse, she had this little dog that was not housebroken. Considering she was staying at home, I felt that this task fell within her domain of domestic chores."

Catherine reached over as if to calm him because she sensed that he was getting a little tense, but all the while he was just readjusting himself in the power chair once again. However, it may be perceived, as she reached over and placed a reassuring hand on his arm as John leaned his head back against the head rest of his chair.

"Well, you were married very early in life" Catherine said as her was busily writing notes. "Was there a reason?" Catherine asked rather pointedly.

John looked over at her. There seemed to be a wisp of hair that kept falling across her forehead. *This actually accentuated her features,* John thought to himself briefly.

"Well, John?" asked Catherine again. *Wonder what is delating his response.*

"I'm not really sure how that applies here." John said rather guardedly.

"I will decide what is applicable and what is not" Catherine said with some force in her voice. *It seems like I have him rather cornered.* Catherine thought to herself while still scribbling notes.

"Well," John began with a little hesitation. After all she was asking a question that has not come up since the spring may be 1975. After taking a sip of water, John continued. "About a year before, when I was a junior in high school, I had gotten her pregnant. I also convinced her to have an abortion. With that I promised to marry her when I graduated from high school."

Catherine sat back and was really quite sure what to say. After a long pause during the early part of this session, she eventually said "I see that is still a tender subject."

"Yes it is, "John said. "I mean, I have changed my viewpoint on the subject since then, and now I realize now that what I did was commit murder, but the Holy Spirit forgave me for those sins of the past."

"My what a crafty soul! I wonder what other secrecy might be hiding?" Questioned Catherine.

"That was the first time 1975 that I even mentioned it. Going any further into that subject I believe we will get totally off-track." John said matter-of-factly. Once we got married, she wanted to have this stupid little dog" , John continued. "all it seemed to do is run around and relieve himself on the carpet or on the newspapers that were haphazardly scattered on the floor." Smiling as if transfixed in some distant memory, "so how bad were the conditions?" John said as he turned his chair slightly so that he would look Catherine straight in the eye, for he had looked away. This was necessary because he could not hold his head in any position accept straightforward for any length of time. In this case Catherine was sitting slightly to the left which really made matters worse because turning his head to the left was the hardest position for him to hold. "How many people do you know that have dog waste on the floor until it turns white?" He said with a level of disgust.

"Well, that would be quite the extreme" remarked Catherine, all the while thinking to herself "*if you're telling me the truth*."

"Fortunately for me at the time I was working two jobs. It was not unusual for me to leave the house around 6 o'clock in the morning and not get home until well after 11 p.m." Shifting his legs, a little while using the hydraulics of the chair. He was able to control the multi-positions by the use of the joystick that rested ever so slightly on his chin. John continued on, "I was doing this, in my mind, to support my wife and child who at the time was only two years old. After all, it was God's intent that the man would work in order to support his family. So, work I did! I worked a good 18 hours a day, sometimes six days a week. When I was not working, I was picking through items that people had placed at the end of their driveway to discard. I would take these items, you see, often fixing them up and turning around and selling them at a garage sale hosted by my mother-in-law. It was just about this time in my life that I began to realize the only way I was going to get ahead in life is if I had some form of a career. Working odd jobs was fine, for the time being, but the long-term effort must be focused more on some type of field of work that I could get into and support my family at a reasonable level as well as provide them with, with what I felt was a decent level of healthcare. To do this I either needed some organization to assist me or I had to find some other means of supporting my family while I focused on building this particular career. Considering I was from a military family, joining the military became an increasingly intriguing idea" John said while taking a sip this time from the straw on his left, suggesting that he was finished with that particular subject. "So, I joined the Army."

"I notice you have two different straws. Are they both for water or do you have something else in the other bottle" Catherine asked inquisitively.

John paused for a moment before continuing. "Right now, I have juice in the one to the left of my head. Sometimes I have coffee first thing in the morning, but right now it is just juice."

"You have or have had anything else in there" questioned Catherine in an attempt to see if he also drank alcohol.

"Normally in this bottle I will only have cranberry juice or coffee. Only first thing in the morning it will be coffee. Sometimes I take a shot of Irish cream. I find that it disrupts my blood pressure, however" John explained.

Not really provided the answer that she was looking for, she rephrased it "what I mean is do you ever put an alcoholic beverage, including beer in your bottle?"

"There may have been a time that I would do such a thing, but I don't drink like that anymore" John explained. "At the time I was working two jobs, as I stated previously, I was gone in excess of 18 hours a day six days a week. I was doing this to support my wife and my two-year-old son. So, there is not much extra money to go around to afford that."

"*He is either very slow to pick up on my suggestions or he's just really slick*" she thought to herself as Catherine scribbled out a few notes on her pad.

"What all are you writing" John asked guardedly.

"Why I am just recording the fact that you say you do not drink alcohol" Catherine responded with a wry smile.

"My very first duty station" John continued, "was Republic of Korea without my wife or child. Most of the other young soldiers would talk about going downtown or the "Ville" as it was so often referred to and mixing with the young ladies. At the time I found this to be something hard to understand but after a while I succumbed to peer pressure and soon found myself doing this as well." John shook his head in acknowledgment and took another sip of water. After drinking a few sips, he cleared his throat and continued. "I rationalized this in my own mind because all of the problems I was having at home. This is not meant as an excuse, but it is just how I rationalized it at the time. This was complicated by the fact my wife seldom wrote although I wrote every day. Six months into my stay overseas, I found that my wife gave birth to another son. It would be another four months before I would see this child."

It was just about at this time that Catherine was dying to interrupt her client and ask pointed questions such as "and how do you think your wife would feel about this?" Or something along these lines. "After all she was at home dealing with one child while pregnant." But rather than breaking her client's concentration she allowed him to continue on.

"Close to my time of being completed overseas," John said rather sensing her irritation. "I got word that my father was dying from cancer. The Red Cross gave me less than 24 hours to get ready to fly home. In my haste I guess I did not have time to separate my life in Korea and I ended up confessing my infidelity to my wife. She, justly so, filed for divorce. After my father's death I found myself so far behind on vacation time that it would be another year and one half before I was able to take any more time off. At this point in time, I was stationed in the western section of Kentucky. So, when my wife decided to file for divorce, I had no way to contest the action in Virginia. Subsequently, I lost all rights to both of my boys."

"So how did that make you feel?" Catherine asked inquisitively.

"It made and continues to make me feel like a real scumbag" replied John immediately. "But that's not why we are here."

John continued to explain "While I was in Kentucky, I met a young Korean woman. She had two children, and her ex-husband was not in her life at all. She had a little boy named Austin who was about five or six when I first meet her. She also had a daughter that was around two years old named Susan. One day I was over at her house relaxing on the couch while she was making dinner. Austin came over to me and asked if he could lay down on the couch as well. I said "certainly" and made room for him. We laid there together for about 10 minutes and then Austin asked me "why don't you push me away like my daddy does." It was at this point that I knew I had found my new home." John stopped and looked over at Catherine and said "yes, yes I know I was looking to compensate my loss of my first two boys by staying with her."

"At any rate," John said "in 1982 I married again for the second time. I was only 25 years old. Both my Korean wife and I were young and still liked to party and have fun. However, my new married life and career stopped allowing me to have as much fun as she wanted to. I continued on with my education; with a goal of first earning a paycheck of at least $1, 000 a month, then, step 2 was to be promoted to Sergeant, and then try to become a military officer. This I accomplished in 1983.

By 1988 my Korean wife and I had 2 more children, a son name Johnny and a daughter named Heather."

"Wait a minute" interrupted Catherine. "I thought the name of your first child was John."

"He is" replied John. "You see I like this name and I wanted it to continue on."

"On?" asked Catherine. "On from what?" "*These men and their ego. Where will it all end*" Catherine question to herself.

"Exactly, but that perhaps can be discussed later" John said then continuing on, "I was also reassigned from Southern Kentucky to southwest Georgia for Officer Candidate School (OCS). After my successful completion of OCS, I was reassigned to Northern Alabama for further training. After this training I went back southwest Georgia for Ranger School. Training was intense but I thoroughly enjoyed it. Until I had the misfortune of blowing out my left knee in the hand-to-hand pit. I was then placed on administrative hold until my orders came to go to Korea. I took my entire family with me, at my expense while I was stationed in Korea. We lived on the local economy. While I was stationed in Korea, I was a Platoon Leader for approximately 30 soldiers. So, the significance of this just meant I was noy home that much."

"So, because you had your family with you, I guess you also lived downtown in this Ville" questioned Catherine. "And while you're pondering that question, were you faithful to your Korean wife?

"Oh, to the contrary." John replied. "My platoon and I spent a good 200 days a year out on maneuvers. My tour of duty in Korea was only 12 months long. I had a return assignment taking me back to Fort Campbell which is in Southwest Kentucky." Coughing a little, John continued. "I served additional three years on Fort Campbell until I received orders to go back to Alabama for additional training. This training cycle was rather typical of the military during my time in the service. I'm not so sure that they still do this type of training and rotation as they did back then."

"And my question with regards to being faithful to your wife? Further, where was your family," asked Catherine inquisitively. *I bet the pig left his family floundering at home, Catherine thought quietly to himself.*

"Although I loved family, I was always on the "hunt" for another woman. Through all of my training my family stayed in my home in Kentucky while I was in training. I would, however, I drove home every weekend for about six months. After the training was over, I was selected to stay in Alabama for a new assignment. Here in this new assignment, I was in charge of a Unit that consisted of 400 men with 13 Drill Sergeants. This new assignment consumed almost all my time."

John cleared his throat before continuing. "By this time" John said as if he was proud, "I was a whiskey drinking, cigar smoking soldier from the 101st Airborne Division and was assigned to a training unit in

Northern Alabama. In this capacity I was never really considered to be a nice guy, hence the nickname my soldiers gave me."

"And what might that be" Catherine asked.

"Hitler," John said. "As a matter of fact, if I had to explain myself in one word, I would probably choose the word philanderer, if nothing else."

"*Interesting choice of words*" Catherine thought to herself rather coldly.

"In my current position in Alabama, I was once again unhappily married with four children, two of which were not my own. It's not that my wife was a bad wife or lady we had merely grown apart. She (my wife at the time) was the same yet I had grown interests far beyond what our marriage was able to support."

"*Interesting choice of words, again*" Catherine continued, all the while tapping her pencil against her teeth rather nervously. *Boy, could I use a cigarette right now.* Catherine thought to herself.

"In this new position I had to be at work no later than 4 o'clock (0400) in the morning. This meant, that I had to leave the house by about 03:15 in the morning. To back this up I had to be in bed by 9 o'clock (2100) every night. I did not get home until about 8 o'clock (2000) at night which limited my amount of time with the family. It did not help that my young daughter (Heather) was allowed to ride her big wheel up and down the hallway outside of my door!"

"I'm sorry because I know I'm not supposed to interrupt, but at this point I have to" said Catherine rather excitedly. "I mean" stammering Catherine realizing that all along she's breaking every ethical code as a social worker "it just seems like you're making excuses to justify your infidelity. Besides, by this point, how many women did you actually have intimate relations with?" Asked Catherine. *I'm rather afraid to ask that question because I'm afraid the answer.*

John looked down again at his useless hands before continuing on. *Nobody ever asked me this before, so here goes* John said to himself before answering her question. "I stopped counting after 15" John responded with a shameful tone.

"You stopped counting after 15!" exclaimed Catherine. "You were quite busy."

John sat there for a moment looking at her with a rather blank look on his face. It started slowly, after all what she said made a lot of sense. Nodding in agreement John said, "Yes, I do believe I was. To answer your other question, yes, I lost count at 15."

"Fifteen" exclaimed Catherine out of sheer astonishment!

John sat there for a moment just staring back at Catherine. He knew at this point no matter what he said this would be exactly what Catherine would be thinking. "*After all, she had me dead to rights!* John thought to himself but chose to continue one anyway. "Yes ma'am" responded John. "But I'm afraid to continue down that line of questioning we will just run off to another painful "rabbit hole."

Catherine, realizing that she was getting off track decided to drop that line of thinking. Then, motioning to John to continue, she said "yes, I agree. Sorry for getting us off track. Please go on Catherine was through her notes really quick and said, "looking at my notes it would appear you were discussing tring to go to sleep in a very busy household."

John sat there for a moment collecting his thoughts before continuing. As if coming to an instant recall, John continued. "My other children had a tendency of always keeping the hall light on to the point where I would get up and turn it off. Eventually, I had to remove the bulb. To add insult to injury my Korean wife decided that she wanted to get a job, so she ended up getting a job at some gambling casino that was in the area. She would leave home around 11 o'clock (2300) at night and not come home until about the time that I got ready to go to work."

"*Sounds to me like she was giving you a taste of your own medicine*" Catherine thought to herself while she shifted slightly in her seat.

John, sensing her level of disdain shifted his position slightly using his chin activated joystick before continuing, "I am not really sure what she did there I just know she would always come home with a very large stack of bills. It was not until much later that I found out she had a separate bank account."

"*Just like all men*" Catherine thought to herself. "*She probably had a separate bank account to keep her money from you*" Catherine thought but this time it brought a smile to her face.

"*I wonder what she's thinking about with that coy smile*" John thought to himself before continuing. "It was along about these times that I received a briefing through the military about the need for more life insurance. So, obtaining more life insurance became something that was first and foremost on my mind. Approximately a month later when I came home from work, I received a phone call. On the other end of the phone was a young lady with a honey dripping southern voice, so I found it hard to say no or to even hang up. She convinced me to have a representative to come by and talk to me about more life insurance. I knew full well that all I was going to get was some fat old, bald-headed man who is going to go over the policy and bore me to tears."

"I see, continue on" Catherine said as she made a few notes.

"Approximately a month later" John continued "I was outside working on my car one day when a young lady came walking down the street. This was not some lady that I could glance at and then look away and never look back."

"*What a pig*" Catherine thought as she continued taking notes. "Do you have a habit of looking at such ladies" she questioned. "*That was a stupid question! Anybody who's been with 15 or more women is always on the hunt!*"

"No, well maybe" John rather stammered. "You see this was a young lady I was captivated with. I mean I could not even look away." John said emphatically. "I just remember looking at the young lady and thinking that it must be nice to have something like that to come to visit. Then she walked up my driveway! It did not take me long to figure out who the owner of the honey dripping voice was that I had spoken to sometime back with regards to life insurance. She was approximately 5 foot 7 and approximately 120 pounds. She had long blonde wavy hair with shimmers of gold and big green eyes that seemed to pull me in. I invited her in, and once I got her settled at the dining table, I went into my bedroom and changed my clothes. I did this is because my clothes were absolutely filthy from working on my car. For the next hour I listened to her explain the different policies. As I sat there and listened to her drone on about insurance, I was just captivated by not only the way she looked but also by her perfume. At this point I don't really remember what she said, she could be selling snake oil for all I knew, I was just focused on one particular freckle on her chest, wondering what it would be like to be able to touch that particular spot. At the time my wife was not interested in any potential policy at all and just laid on the couch smoking cigarettes. Too no surprise, I purchased a policy from the young lady."

"*I bet you did and to think he was doing this right in front of his wife! What a pig!*" Catherine thought to herself as she continued writing. "Continue on," stammered Catherine as she motioned with her pencil for John to continue.

"About a month later, something possessed me to give this young insurance lady a call. To my surprise she said something to the effect that she had been wanting to call me as well because she got the policy in. Normally, she went on to explain that when these policies came in, she liked to sit down with the client and review the policy to clear up any extenuating questions that there might be. We both agreed on a lunch meeting which I listed on my calendar as a lunch date. We met up at a local restaurant and she was full of personal questions about my family and education. I did not really understand at the time why she had so many questions but when we parted, I remember that she showed me her hotel room key."

"*And I'm sure you were Mr. Innocent!*" Catherine thought to herself.

"I thought for quite some time about the key and why she showed it to me"

"*Truly a pig!*" Catherine again said to herself while shaking her head.

John said without losing a beat. "About another month went by before I decided to follow up on our lunch meeting and arranged to go by to see her at her hotel room. I went and saw her one evening on my way back from checking up on a soldier's family. The young soldier was training in my unit, and he did not receive pay.

"Why did he not receive any pay" Catherine asked.

"There was a problem with finance, or something like that. It's not uncommon" John proceeded. "At any rate, after I dropped off food with the soldier's family, I picked up two beers and thought maybe I would stop by the insurance ladies' room to watch the end of Monday Night Football. When I got up to her room, she informed me that she did not drink beer and she did not like football. So, we ended up talking a little bit and I just found myself being drawn in more and more."

Catherine interjected once again by saying "that should have been your clue that something was amiss."

"OH, I certainly agree, now that I know how it all played out" John remarked. "But that was not too clear to me then. I just remember that before the end of our conversation I asked her if I would be able to kiss her. She said something to the effect of yes. Her lips were as sweet and as intoxicating as new wine. The rest was history..." John then allowed his words to trail off.

"Just to be sure," John added as if to qualify his earlier statement. "I first met Mercedes,

"Wait a minute" Catherine interjected. "You mean to tell me her name was Mercedes" Catherine asked inquisitively.

"Yes, why do you ask" John responded with a blank look on his face.

"No, nothing" responded Catherine all the while thinking to herself *"what a convenient name. Sounds more like an exotic dancer."*

"I met her originally approximately August or September 1989. At the time I had four children that lived with me, two of these children were my Korean wife's from a previous marriage.

"Typical, here he brought her over from Korea and now he's talking about abandoning her" Catherine thought to herself with disgust!

"At this point in time" John continued oblivious to Catherine's inner thoughts. "I had been the father figure for these two children for approximately nine years, ever since I met her while I lived in Kentucky."

"So, you met this Korean woman while you were living in Kentucky" questioned Catherine.

"Why yes," said John. "I did not bring her from overseas, if that's what you were thinking. As a matter fact we were living together, and the issue of marriage never came up. It was only after the Army started to inquire as to why she did not have a military ID card under my name that the issue of marriage ever came up. But that's a whole different story and I do not wish to delve into because it would just get everything off track."

"Well, you are probably correct, and we would not want to do that" agreed Catherine. Catherine then shifted her legs before picking up the pitcher of water that was in front of her and pouring a glass. After taking a sip she placed her glass down on the appropriate coaster, "don't let me stop you, please continue."

"The other two children were a result of my marriage to my Korean wife" explained John. "Their names are Johnny (John IV) and Heather. I also had two children from a previous marriage that lived in Virginia. These two children are named Johnny (John III) and Mark. I was currently paying child support for these two."

"Wait a minute" Catherine interjected. "So, you have two children named after you" questioned Catherine in an attempt to clarify.

"That's correct" nodded John with approval.

"Okay, I just wanted to clarify" stated Catherine as she continued writing in her notes all the while thinking to herself "*unbelievable!*"

Again, John grabbed his straw in his teeth and took a sip. He swallowed the water slowly before continuing on. "Mercedes had been married once before and had two children as a result of her marriage. These two children were named Angela and Tammy.

In December 1989 Mercedes decided to move back with her ex-husband who was then living in Austin, Texas. At the time, this was devastating to me. Even though, at the time, I was currently married I was totally enamored with Mercedes. I could not get her out of my head. It was as if I had a craving where I could not see enough of her. During this time, I was also up for some additional professional development training which was conducted at a different post. As such, I was temporarily reassigned to Fort Leavenworth, Kansas for approximately three months and then I returned to Alabama. While I was in Kansas, I made up my mind that I wanted to divorce my Korean wife. My divorce was finalized somewhere between March and May 1990. Once I told Mercedes of my divorce she subsequently moved back to Alabama from Texas.

We got married the following August. It was right around this time and right before we were married that her father had become injured while on the job down in Florida. For some reason she felt compelled to run down to Florida and see him before he went in for back surgery. After the short little trip down to Florida, she came back, and we were married on the 16th. We had a wonderful honeymoon in the Poconos, and it was during this time she let me know more of what she was doing when she was down visiting her father in Florida. She told me that while she was in Florida her ex-husband just happened to be down there on a visit. He was trying to talk her out of getting married again and in doing so, they shared a bath together!"

"He is actually shocked!" Catherine thought to herself in amazement.

"When we went into this marriage, I had the delusion that we would be able to blend all six children together. I knew it would be hard at first" John continued after taking yet another sip of water through the straw "but I still felt that it was "doable."

"Of course, you thought that way. After all, I'm sure you think that raising children is women's work" Catherine thought to herself while allowing John to continue.

"After all the two oldest girls (Angela and Susan) were approximately the same age and were in the same grade. Austin was older and was in high school. Because I had raised both Austin and Susan for about 9 years, I did not have any real concerns with those two. They both had asked to stay with me after I divorced their mother who had subsequently moved to Seattle, Washington. Johnny and Tammy were also similar in age, and both were in elementary school one grade apart. Heather was approximately three years old. Our house was tight, to say the least, but still comfortable and every child had their own assignment and assigned room.

Shortly after Labor Day I was at work as a Commander for an Advanced Individual Training (AIT) company on Fort McClellan, Alabama. I was confronted with divorce papers delivered by the same Military Police (MP) that I had worked very closely with." John said while shaking his head in disbelief.

"I guess you got a taste of your own medicine" Catherine thought to herself while she collected her own thoughts and then asked, "how did that make you feel?"

"I took this as a HUGE slap in my face" John explained. "Having this done by the very people I have worked with (meaning the MPs) was truly embarrassing. Mercedes, my current wife, decided to file divorce papers because she said she could not handle all of the children in the house. Mercedes demanded that I get rid of the two children that were my ex-wife's and send my two children that I had won during child custody hearings back to my ex-wife! This was the price I had to pay in order for Mercedes to stop the divorce action."

"*It is remarkable that a man would want to keep the children*" Catherine thought to herself while motioning on for John to continue.

"I remember literally pleading with her" John said as he adjusted himself in his chair by moving joystick. "I mean I literally had to plead with her not to make me send back my son, but she would not hear of it."

"Wait a minute, I'm confused" Catherine questioned. "If she wanted to you to be without your children, yet you say you wanted to be with them, why didn't you just allow her to go along with the divorce action?"

"It was quite simple" John began. "If I was to allow her to get the divorce, at this point, then all of my efforts up until this would have been in vain and I really would have destroyed my career much more so than possibly was already" John explained before continuing.

"I ended up sending back all four of these children. It was rather interesting because this was the second marriage that was dissolved and the second time, I had to say goodbye to my children. Almost as if it was ordained. By December 1990 Mercedes found out she was pregnant! So perhaps my having to get rid of my other four children was just a way of making room for this new child that would be entering into my house. Then when I found out the news that she was pregnant with twins, I was overwhelmed with joy! It was that time that I made a silent pledge to myself that these two new children would never leave my side." John said matter-of-factly.

"Wait a minute" Catherine interjected. "So, she was pregnant with twins? How did that happen? Do twins run in your family?"

"Well, the short answer to that is no; twins do not run in my family" John stated again matter-of-factly. "It was kind of funny actually," John said with a smile. "You see we were getting an ultrasound at the time and the medical technician that was performing the ultrasound just got up and started to leave the room. I stopped him and said, "where are you going?" He responded by saying "well sir there always has to be two technicians in here for the ultrasound when there are twins."

"Given the circumstances I thought this was tremendously funny" John said with a laugh.

"And how did she take it" Catherine asked.

"Actually, she started to cry" John explained shaking his head again in disbelief.

John once again took a sip of water through the straw before continuing. "When they were born, which was prematurely by several weeks, they were both in respiratory distress. The military med-evaced them by ground ambulance to Birmingham which was about an hour away by car. You see it was dark and stormy that night, literally; so bad were the conditions that the standard helicopter method was not possible. As a matter fact both babies were whisked away so quickly that Mercedes didn't even have a chance to hold them. Once I was sure that Mercedes was stabilized, I followed the ambulance into Birmingham. Upon arrival I found both babies resting quietly in small incubators. I asked the doctor that night if they were going to make it. I just remember him saying something to the effect of "if they last the night then they will be just fine."

"That seems rather cold" interjected Catherine.

"My thoughts exactly" John said. "I just figured it was because he was a doctor in the infant intensive care unit (ICU) and was used two dealing with this type of situation. I guess in a way of breaking the ice, the doctor suggested that I follow him downstairs for cup of coffee. I went with him and we had just a rather pleasant conversation until we both return to the ICU floor. Before I left that night I went over to where both babies were. I let each of them hold my little finger. How big my finger was compared to their hand" John said and seemed to rather drift off in some form of remembrance. "I mean these were my boys, I had lost two so long ago, and this time I was not going to leave these boys. So, I made a silent pledge to ensure that I would take care of them all their life and I would be there for them regardless of any trials or tribulations that I may have to go through to ensure that this was accomplished. I followed up on this promise later on in life by telling them both on numerous occasions that no matter where I lived there would always be a home for them." John was obviously showing signs of stress at this point with tears beginning to stream down his face.

"*He even has tears in his eyes. I don't think I have ever met somebody like this, a man that is this passionate about his children, very interesting. This is perhaps rather refreshing*" Catherine thought to herself before allowing him to continue.

"Sorry," John said. "I don't mean to do that for pity's sake," John explained. "Ever since my MS got worse, I find it hard to control my emotions" John further explained. "Would you mind giving me a tissue and wiping my eyes" John asked.

"Certainly" Catherine said as she reached for an available tissue. Standing up she walked over and wiped his eyes gently. "There, is that better" Catherine asked in almost a motherly tone.

"Yes, quite" John responded. "Thank you" he said before continuing. "By this time in my marriage I found myself getting increasingly secluded. I had several friends at the same military installation as myself, yet they no longer wanted to have anything to do with me. Several of these friends I had known for quite some time, male and female alike. I remember Mercedes telling me that men and women cannot be friends because sex always got in the way. At any rate, Mercedes did not want me to have anything to do with these friends anyway."

"Didn't you find this rather odd" Catherine asked inquisitively.

"Yes, I did, as a matter fact. But you see she had a way about her that even if it didn't make sense, you still kind of wanted to go along with what she was saying" John explained with a somewhat of a confused look on his face.

"*What an interesting look. It is as if he doesn't know why he's even thinking this way*" Catherine thought to herself all the while chewing on the end of her pencil.

Continuing on in totally oblivion to Catherine's thoughts, John continued "By the end of April 1992 I was on orders for Alaska. I had to report by July 4 and could not leave until the first day after Memorial Day. My household furniture, however, had to leave by May 1. This was to ensure that my household furniture was available in Alaska when I arrived. This meant that I had to stay in temporary dwellings off post for almost 30 days! Fortunately for me I owned two trailers downtown and I was able to move into one. In the meantime, Mercedes decided that she would reopen her divorce case with her ex-husband to sue for more child support."

"So, I take it she stopped her action against you and I guess she started up action against her ex-husband, am I getting this correct" Catherine asked in order to clarify the subject in her own mind.

John nodded in approval before continuing. "Her ex-husband decided to counter-sue for custody of her two minor children." This sent Mercedes off into a spiral! She soon focused all her attention on the countersuit rather than her own lawsuit. She had to pay $5000 down to her attorney which she did not have. I was the only one working at the time. She ended up losing her lawsuit and had to pay her ex-husband $150 a month which meant that it came out of my paycheck!"

"Wait a minute" Catherine once again interjected. "You mean to tell me that the judge in Alabama ruled that she had to pay $150 per month even though she did not have a job?"

"You got it!" John said. "It was ruled that because she had a bachelor's degree, she was now able to get a job, assuming one arose. On top of this Mercedes's oldest daughter went to live with her father (Mercedes's ex-husband)."

"So, after all of this, the only thing that came out of it was that you had one less child to care for yet you had to pay out $150 a month from your own paycheck to pay for her child support" Catherine asked to clarify herself yet all the while in disbelief.

"That's about the size of it" John said in agreement. Continuing he explained further, "We moved to Alaska after camping in a tent along the way for 33 days. Shortly after arrival at my new duty station I thought it would be interesting to take the family on a drive to see a herd of wild buffalo. We drove out onto the testing ranges which was approximately 15 miles from the nearest building. While we were driving, I noticed a problem with my van. Smoke started to come up from under the hood. On closer inspection I found that the wiring harness burned up. This meant I would have extensive auto repairs. However, my immediate problem was how to get home. It was near four o-clock in the afternoon, and I had two children in grades two and three and two babies that were almost a year old. The only way to get back was to walk. This is what we did, but unfortunately our path took us right through the herd of wild buffalo! We walked through silently although one large buffalo was certainly looking at us. This particular buffalo started snorting and pawing the ground! If this buffalo decided to charge, we had no place to go, no tree to climb, the only thing that got us through was prayer. Fortunately, God shined on us that day and we got through the herd without incident. It is obvious to me now that it was God's grace that allowed us to walk through this herd without one word from my two baby boys. We ended up walking approximately 7 or 8 miles before I found a telephone pole with a range phone attached to it. I was able to get in touch with my NCO (noncommissioned officer that worked for me) and he was able to come out and rescue us."

"Gosh" Catherine said in astonishment. "You're lucky to get out of there and you are lucky that you had this individual to call."

"I agree" John said before continuing. "I made the appropriate arrangements and had my van towed to the only repair shop in town. The repairs were quite extensive and expensive. Within about six months of suffering through these extensive car repairs, Mercedes was notified that her daughter, the one who was living with her father in New Jersey." John explained "was in a youth Psychiatric Institute in New Jersey. This was the oldest daughter that insisted on being with her father rather than living with us in Alaska. Upon hearing this news, Mercedes insisted on immediately flying to New Jersey to rescue her daughter. This caused me to have to take out a personal loan at 31% interest to pay for her round-trip plane ticket and her daughter's one way ticket from New Jersey to Alaska. It also meant that while I was active-duty military I also had to raise four children, two of which were in high chairs. I did so efficiently for two weeks. When Mercedes returned home with her daughter, the daughter immediately thought that I was the bad guy! While I lived in Alaska there were problems with the children from my ex-marriage and Mercedes's daughter constantly caused problems including hanging out in the barracks with enlisted soldiers sent to Alaska for training from the lower 48. All of this, in the eyes of the military, did not go well. While all this was going on my first wife, my high school sweetheart from Virginia, called and said that she was having problems with my two oldest sons. She wanted to know if they could come to Alaska and live with me. I immediately said yes. Now to be sure I must enter in this one caveat, all I ever wanted to do was have a son that I could raise and spend time with. I believe I got this because my father was a Marine and was gone too many times. One of the major reasons for me joining the Army rather than the Marines was that I wanted to be home to help raise my son. I let that first relationship slip away due to my own stupid indiscretions. I reestablished my life with my Korean wife, from whom I had two more children. Once again through my stupid, ignorant indiscretions I hurt a very dear woman and I lost my other two children. Even though I was now remarried to someone that I was infatuated with, and we had two children, I still had this overwhelming desire" John said yet allowing his words to drift off as if the thought was not continued. "There was this overwhelming desire all balled up inside me" John continued to explain "that kept gnawing at me all these years, to reconnect with my first two sons. This had been a major focus in my mind ever since I had lost them in 1979. Gaining my two sons back had actually been a topic of discussion with my Korean wife as well. She turned the idea down cold. This now was an opportunity that I could raise my two sons from so long ago. I accepted, probably before I realized or could've fathomed the potential outcome."

"So, you got your two boys back from your first marriage. How did this workout" Catherine asked once again inquisitively. All the while she kept thinking to herself "*what type of a man places this type of importance on having children, yet he can't seem to hold onto a wife?*"

A little but more comfortable with himself at this point, John readjusted his legs before continuing. "With a future assignment of going to Germany I ended up taking an early retirement primarily so that Mercedes's oldest daughter would not have to graduate from high school overseas. So, I retired on 1 August 1994 and moved to Lakeland, Florida which was Mercedes's childhood home. Probably one of my larger mistakes at this point was continuing to practice that well-established practice in the military in that the wife would handle all financial matters. Within two years of retirement, I was bankrupt! Perhaps I would not have been if I was in charge of all the finances."

"Perhaps you should have been or at least aware of what was going out" Catherine interjected, once more.

"Perhaps" John said. "I raised this suggestion only to be faced with extreme resistance and threats of divorce to the point where if I was to follow up on this action of taking over the finances it could possibly mean losing my family. It was because of this I allowed her to retain control over the house finances. Throughout this whole time, I worked diligently to provide the best home I could. I rationalized it in my own mind as that if I lost this family, it would not be any of my doing. Therefore, not only did I take care of the outside of the house, but I also cleaned the inside the house as well. Now when I mean that I cleaned the inside of the house, I mean that I took care of the laundry, changing beds, making sure that the children had a bath, washed dishes, vacuum the carpet, dusted, and even mop floors."

"He really seems committed to this particular marriage; I wonder what changed" Catherine thought. "Do go on" she said motioning with her hand for John to continue.

Understanding her sense of desire for him to continue, John once again took a sip of water and then continued in his soliloquy. "In addition to this I ended up cooking a large portion of the meals, and generally took care of the children which included taking them to their doctor/ dental appointments as well as working two jobs!

We lived quite well" he explained. "I mean it wasn't perfect, I wasn't perfect, but I did the best I could with what I had. At any rate, I thought it was a happy family. Prior to this Mercedes had a job that required her travel to Mexico quite frequently. While she was gone, I fell into the mold of caring for Daniel and David and their older half-sister Tammy. I fit into this role despite having a full-time job at the city of Lakeland and teaching school at night. When Tammy had her senior prom, Mercedes was not home for this, and I took the pictures! Every morning I would make bacon and eggs for everyone, all including Mercedes, whenever she was home. On Valentine's Day I even made heart-shaped pancakes" John said as he let his voice rather drift off.

Just as Catherine was going to interject to bring him back on track, John began again. "Often, I would wait at the foot of the stairs and call to her that breakfast was ready. But in 2004 all this changed. This is when the devil set in!"

"Why do you say that" Catherine asked.

"If I answer that question right now it will divert me off the subject and I do not wish to lose momentum. Besides" John paused for a minute for another sip of water "In order to tell the tale of 2004 I need to digress to shortly after Christmas 2003. Traditionally we always went out for New Year's Eve. We always liked to find a venue that would offer a dinner, dancing and hotel room all in one spot. We had not planned on going out on December 31, 2003, but then Mercedes changed her mind. So, after Christmas, we started looking online for places to go, but we seem to be too late and that there were no vacancies! Then Mercedes found a site called *Interlude* which was a site that looked eerily like a site for Swingers without coming right out of the same so."

"So was this really a Swinger's site" question Catherine.

"Wait" John cautioned. "I'll get to that part. When we first got to the hotel where the party was, we got our key and went to the room. The room had two double beds in it, which I found of interest. Just as we were getting settled in, another couple, somewhat younger than we were, came in the room, much to everyone's surprise! In my normal way of joking at things, I said something to the effect of "well I know what the other set of double beds is for" John said with a sly smile. This other couple was not nearly as amused as I was. The gentleman said something to the effect that he thought the room was overbooked as they departed. Later, we were having a casual cocktail when we were approached by a well-dressed gentleman who called himself Dr. Bob. He started to talk to me about the "lifestyle." The more he talked to me about this, the more I did not like it. Finally, I asked him if there was a pentagram painted on the dancefloor. He was not amused by my level of humor.

During the course of the evening" John continued to explain "the party became more intense, to the point to where everyone seemed electrified! What I mean by that was there was a sense of energy and everyone seemed to be feeding off of each other. I got up to get champagne for our midnight toast in which case it was 10 minutes to the hour there was already a long line. While I was standing in line, I happened to notice a young lady directly behind me. She was dressed in nothing more than clear plastic wrap without any form of undergarments. I complimented her on her dress and then forced myself not to watch her anymore. By the time I got back to my table there was another young lady sitting there. I excused myself and sat down in my chair only to see Mercedes up on the dancefloor dancing with some guy. The young lady next to me started talking and told me that he was her husband and he found Mercedes to be very pleasant. She continued on until finally I understood that she was interested in me. I told her that I was on my third marriage and although

I appreciated her offer, I would have to decline because I wanted nothing to mess up this marriage."

It was at this point Catherine interjected "this was rather new for you, wasn't it? I mean given your past history I would think that this would be somewhere that you would feel quite at home."

John just sat there for a minute looking somewhat perplexed. "Well yes given my past one may assume so, but that was far from the case" John explained. "See for the most part I had very solid conservative views."

Continuing on John further explained that "after the party I was riddled with all kinds of questions about this particular form of lifestyle, which is what they called it. I remember telling Mercedes that I just couldn't understand how people could live this way. Unfortunately, Mercedes took my inquisitiveness to heart and insisted on joining this club. She swore that would only be until she turned 50 which was in 2006. She was constantly in demand and answering instant messages from all kinds of different men and did not understand why I was upset by it. I remember asking her if I had wronged her in some fashion because I could not understand her behavior. As an explanation for her actions, she referred back to an incident which I will say was Easter 1992. We all had planned on going to Easter Sunrise Service in 1992. When I say we, it consisted of Mercedes and I, both of Mercedes's daughters (my stepchildren), my two children from a previous marriage (Johnny and Heather) along with Daniel and David. Everybody was already to go and then the two stepdaughters decided they did not want to go. So, I told Mercedes that I would just go and take Daniel and David, Johnny and Heather. My wife threw a fit that I would suggest taking our sons! This really threw me for a loop because I could not understand how anybody would object so violently going to an Easter Sunrise Service! She refused to let me take both Daniel and David who at the time were only about nine or 10 months old. So, I took both Johnny and Heather to the Easter Sunrise Service. When I got back home everything was fine except Mercedes insisted that I was choosing my two children from a former marriage over our two children. I just diffused this argument by not gratifying it with a response. So now flash forward to 2004 she decided that because I had the audacity to go to Easter Sunrise Service in 1992 there was justification for her current behavior in joining the Swingers club! I was flabbergasted to say the least!"

By this time Catherine had a world wind worth of questions but she chose not to ask any of them but rather just let John vent because he was certainly a role. "Continue on" said Catherine motioning with her hands.

"May 2004" John continued, "I literally had enough, and I wanted to make the divorce as painless as possible. So, I went to a legal assistance office where the divorce would cost $75. At the time I was attending an annual conference for storm preparation in Tampa, Florida. I left the conference early. I picked up my wife from work and went to a small park in the local city. We shared lunch and then I shared my concerns about her behavior and asked her for divorce. Of course, she flatly refused to have any discussion of a divorce. I had explained to her that I had placed her on a pedestal and that I did not expect this type of behavior from her. She told me that was my mistake because she should not be on a pedestal. At the time I disagreed, but in retrospect I should have listened. I continued to press my argument and I told her I wanted the divorce to be as amicable as possible but she refused a discussion on any account. In retrospect, this was probably the root of my entire problem with Mercedes. I placed her on a pedestal and ended up worshiping her as a goddess rather than directing my attentions to the proper God.

For the next several nights I remember helping my sons with their homework and seeing their two blonde heads bending down at the kitchen counter and thinking to myself I lost two children in my first marriage, lost my two children from my second marriage and now I am faced with losing these two children! I thought about my decision for quite some time. I then remembered the vow that I made to each one of these boys back when they were in the hospital in Birmingham, Alabama when they were first born. At that time, I remember clasping their little hand around my little finger and making the vow that I would never leave them and that I would always be there to take care of them. After many days of considering everything, I made the decision to endeavor to persevere and hopefully she would stay true to her word and stop in 2006."

"You're taking a mighty big step and a dangerous one" Catherine advised.

"I know or at least I know that now" John explained. "But I really believed that my marriage was strong enough to endure even though I was a quadriplegic. I also had this inner feeling that kept telling me that she would end up doing it anyway because that's just the way she was."

"And you knew this or at least had the inclination that something like this may occur from the very beginning" questioned Catherine as she leaned forward in her chair.

"Yeah, pretty much" John said rather matter-of-factly.

"Amazing" Catherine remarked while shaking her head. "Well, please continue."

"It must be understood" John began "that for all this time my health was deteriorating to the point where it was noticeable. In 1997 I started to experience numbness and tingling in my left leg and foot. This feeling soon progressed to the point where whenever I would take a shower and close my eyes, I would have to hold onto the wall, or I would lose my balance and fall over. This got a little bit more serious when as a function of my job I would have to look up to observe things or to take a picture of something. Whenever I would look up like this" John said while leaning his head back as far as he could considering the limitations of his power chair headrest. He did this to demonstrate how he had to lean back. Continuing John said "I would have to hold onto a wall or a similar structure. If I did not, I would lose my balance. I remember vividly that in 2002 my sons were getting ready to start their recreational soccer league season. They were interested in improving their running capability. I thought it would be fun if we went out and ran together every morning. This was not something unusual for me to do after a career in the military and it was something that I wanted to get back into doing. We started out slow and would just run around our small neighborhood which was not even a half a mile. After the first day, I remember complaining about my left foot and feeling like somebody had tied a brick to it! Right about the same time, I would go out and attempt to walk around a major lake in our area. All the way around this lake was approximately 3 miles. I would not even get one quarter of the way around this lake and my left leg would totally go out on me! On other occasions if I walked too quickly, I would often end up tripping over my own foot. When I went to the doctor and described this abnormality, they would just tell me that when this occurred call 911 and go to the hospital to get a blood test so that they might have those results on record" John said with a nod. "As part of this whole process I had developed a symptom of drop foot."

"What is drop foot" Catherine asked inquisitively or at least as a way to stay in the conversation and as a way to get John to keep talking more and more.

"It occurs when you pick up your foot" John explained "and your nerves do not get the message to hold up your toes. Your toes drop down and you end up scraping the top of your foot along the surface of which you are walking on, hence the term drop foot. This condition also increases your chance of tripping. To help alleviate this problem I started wearing a device that strapped around my lower leg and through a series of Bluetooth devices and a pressure switch in my shoe, my drop foot was controlled to a certain extent. The device you see," John attempted to explain "would send an electrical impulse to my foot causing the toes to raise up to a near-normal position. It was still dangerous for me to walk, however, especially when I tried to walk as quickly as I used to. I would end up tripping over my own foot and falling, normally with a very loud "thump." To assist in walking I would use a cane. I had a very nice selection of canes, but every time I fell even these it took a toll on my dignity as well as the canes themselves. I guess I should've gone with more of a medical device; but I preferred to use dress canes so that I could maintain some form of dignity. I just wasn't ready to give up."

"Yes vanity, one of the deadly sins" commented Catherine as she motioned for John to continue.

"True" John said while nodding in agreement. "There were other occasions, especially at night in the house that I would walk around the corner of my couch all the while using my couch to lean on so as not to lose my balance and falling on the floor. Normally, on these occasions I would be able to pull myself up. But as my illness got worse, I would find that I did not have the energy pull myself up right away. So it was on these occasions that I would frequently just sit on the floor until I had rested for a given period of time. Sometimes this can be 15 minutes, other times it could be over an hour."

"And how did this make you feel" Catherine questioned. She already had a pretty good idea but as part of active listening she wanted to keep John engaged in the conversation as much as she could.

"How do you think it made me feel" John exclaimed. "It may me feel like a fool, a very vulnerable fool."

"Interesting choice of words" Catherine said. "Do go on."

John again took a draw on the straw before continuing. "To compound my medical problems even further, I developed asthma in 2004. I remember waking up early one morning, possibly around 4 AM, and thinking that someone had come into the room and sucked out all the oxygen from the room. After my head cleared the fog of sleep away, I realize this proposition was ridiculous because my wife, who was lying next to me, appeared to be breathing just fine. So, I got up and went downstairs into our family room and sat in my recliner. By this time, I also had developed a never-ending hacking dry cough. So, I sat there in my recliner leaning over with my head in my hands, coughing almost continuously until it suddenly stopped almost as quickly as it had set in. This went on, night after night, this way me, staying downstairs so that my incessant coughing would not wake up my wife. I went several times to the doctor receiving stronger and stronger cough medication. I'd even gotten up to the point where I was prescribed cough medication laced with codeine. So, in the evening my routine would be after drinking numerous cocktails of Jim Beam® and Diet Coke® at about a 50-50 mixture, I would take a shot of NyQuil®, then wash it all down with a shot of my codeine laced cough syrup and nestle down into my easy chair. I would get about two or three hours of sleep before the coughing would start up again."

"Do you realize how dangerous that was" Catherine interjected.

"I knew it was not overly smart but at the same time I was growing desperate" John explained. "This regime went on for about five months until finally the military doctors sent me for further evaluation. The result of this rendered the determination that I had developed asthma/COPD. Neither one of these were surprising because I had smoked for 27 years. At the time that I stopped smoking I was smoking about two packs of cigarettes a day along with five cigars, on the average. After this diagnosis the doctor prescribed three different asthma medications which has seem to have halted or arrested the advancement. In this regard, I consider myself a lucky one.

Further compounding my medical problems, I developed lower back problems. These problems became so severe that even if I stood up for short period of time, I would end up bending forward at the waist. This made it very difficult for me to stand for any length of time which limited my ability to cook which is something I dearly like to but the pain in my back was so severe that I had to put a pillow behind me whenever I sat down. By this time, I was also eating 800 mg prescription strength ibuprofen as if these were M&M's® at least four times a day with no relief in sight" John further explained. "Often times I would lay awake at night in bed, restless because I could not get any pain relief. All this time Mercedes kept telling me that I had MS, but I did not want to hear this because I remember my father having this disease. Based on those memories, I did not want to go through what I saw him go through."

"Let me get this straight, your father had MS so you knew, at least to some extent, how bad this disease could get" questioned Catherine just so she could make sure her notes were correct.

"Yep, pretty much" John said. "You see my father died of cancer before the MS got too bad. So, I really didn't have a good idea of exactly how devastating this disease could be. But I was determined to continue going to the doctor until I had a diagnosis. By this time, I had already gone through numerous neurologists without any adequate answers. So, I decided to fire my current neurologist from the University of South Florida and I asked the military to assign yet another neurologist. I waited diligently for the mail to arrive, which took about three weeks. Once I got my authorization for yet another neurologist, I hurried up and made an appointment. Now mind you, throughout this whole time I was working full-time, and teaching school at night for three different colleges (two of which were online). I had also developed increasing difficulties to the extent that if all the lights were out in the room, I would totally lose my bearings and fall. I was in total denial yet at the same time I remember making a New Year's Eve resolution that I would either "defeat what had afflicted me or succumb to it."

"*Again, an interesting choice of words*" Catherine thought to herself quietly. "Do go on" Catherine said as she continued to write. "I realized my writing is rather old school, but it's a technique that I learned while in school that helps me to retain information all the while getting a better feel for my client."

"I went to this new neurologist" John explained "and after a series of tests I was informed that the MS was in my spine, but I also had problems of another nature in my spine. The MS was in my cervical spine and that I had a bulging disc as well as degenerative discs in my lumbar spine which could be operated on. So, in time, I believe 2009, I had laser spine surgery from which, upon recovery I no longer had the pain and most of the numbness in my left leg was totally gone, including the bending over severely at the waist after a short period of standing. It was all gone. Unfortunately, and much to my demise, all my other problems remained. If this was not enough within about six months of having successful back surgery, I fell and broke three ribs! As a result of this and while my ribs were healing, I started to use my power chair more often.

I was still going to see my back doctor for post-surgery evaluation and the doctor told me not to rely so heavily on the power chair because if I did, I would be condemned to using it for good. I explained to him that I was only using it because I was afraid of walking and falling while my ribs were still healing. Regardless, the last time I stood and attempted to walk was Thanksgiving morning 2012. I remember this clearly because I had been up preparing the turkey for Thanksgiving dinner and went to go to the bathroom and fell on the floor. Mercedes had to call 911 to get the EMTs out to stand me up and put me back in my chair. By 2013 I had my first pulmonary embolism and after eight days in the hospital I had lost the ability to stand on my own and have been in my power chair ever since.

By 2014 my MS had progressed to the extent that we had to move out of my house that I had lived in since the year 2000. We moved into a smaller home, but one that I could get around in much easier. By August of the same year my son informed me that my loving wife of nearly 25 years had a boyfriend. He, my son, showed me computer files where my wife had been sending naked pictures of herself to two different men. It was right around this time frame that my wife told me that she had to have sex again. When she first told me this, I went silent for a period of time. I thought about this long and hard because after all even though I was unable to do anything like this, why would I wish a similar fate on my loved ones? So, after quite a bit of time considering this, I came to the realization that if my answer was no, she would do anyway behind my back. Based on her past performance, this is usually the way she will operate. With a heavy sigh my answer was "as long as you only do it once a month and I do not know anything about it, I guess that would be "okay" or words to this effect."

Catherine sat back in her chair, and after re-crossing her legs she said "this was rather magnanimous of you. I mean that allowing her to do this discreetly would've been a major concession in any marriage and it speaks quite highly of you and obviously the love you had for this woman."

John once again shifted his legs by using the joystick that he held up near his mouth. "I adored her so much to the point of holding her up as an idol. I just could not say no to almost anything she asked. It's not that I was perfect," John said as his mind was obviously drifting in some form of melancholy trance. "Why even her scent, minus any perfume, was intoxicating! And her skin was softer than anything I've ever felt. The best way I can compare this would be, to the flower petal of a lily. I know that this analogy may sound strange," then John paused for a moment and looked away. "I just never felt anything like it. She literally had full control. Little did I know that her personality was more like a Venus fly trap."

"How was that" Catherine said.

To quell her curiosity, John merely replied "she lures you in then she eats her prey."

"Apparently. Again, please continue. Oh, wait a minute" Catherine suddenly said while looking at her watch. "I hate to say this, but our time is up. Having said this, though, I really feel the need to schedule another appointment. Would you agree to that" she asked.

"I believe I can do that if the appointments are set for the early afternoon. You see it will take that long for me to get here because I live quite some distance away" John explained.

CHAPTER TWO

...The Vicious Truth

About two weeks went by before his next appointment. Once again, he arrived several minutes early and waited out in the waiting room. He made himself comfortable, the best a quadriplegic confined to a power chair could. As part of this process, he rocked his chair back. In this position he could get his feet slightly higher than his head. Once he was in the proper position, John settled in for what may be a long wait. After what seemed to be an eternity, 15 minutes, a young female voice called his name, thus breaking the silence.

"Sir, sir" the young girl said as she gently shook his shoulder. "The doctor will see you now."

John opened his eyes and he saw a young girl standing beside him dressed in the standard light blue "scrubs" that all medical personnel seem to wear. She had long blonde hair that was braided into a single braid that she had draped across her shoulder. She was clutching onto his chart, what appeared to be for dear life, when she said "please go to the first door on the left. The doctor will be in shortly."

John responded with acknowledgment and lowered his chair. Once his chair was lowered appropriately, he drove into the appropriate spot and settled in to wait. He wasn't in the office very long until Catherine arrived. When she came into the office, she acted like she was very much frazzled and smelled of cigarette smoke.

"I'm sorry I'm late" she said as she placed a series of papers that she was holding on the desk in front of her. "My last patient ran a little bit longer than I was expecting" she said as she brushed one strand of hair out of her face. "Now where were we?"

"I was telling you about my life" John reminded her.

She inserted her VA issued ID card into the computer keyboard tray which was necessary for her to gain access to her records. Manipulating the keyboard, she soon pulled up his records. After a brief read, she turned around and said, "ah yes, you were telling me about life with your ex-wife."

"Yes" John said as he made himself comfortable once again in his chair. After taking a sip of water from his straw, John said "where did I leave off?"

"Let me look" Catherine said, and she started scrolling through her notes. "Here I have it, you were talking about how you had just given your wife permission to have sex with other people."

"Ah, yes. Quite right" John said moving his head back and forth in agreement. "Well, let me tell you it did not take very long before she made known her activities which started out immediately. It was obvious what she was doing, which was totally against everything that we had just talked about." John said while glancing down at his useless hands. "I remember in the very beginning she would go in and pack a bag and get all dressed up. I was so bothered by these actions that I would leave the house and drive my power chair down the street until after she left. I remember having numerous arguments about her behavior. One argument in the beginning started when she came in the house door, just after arriving home from her boyfriend's and an all-night tryst. Without washing her hands, she tried to give me my morning pills. I started yelling and screaming and telling her that I wanted her to wash her hands first because I did not know where her hands had been."

"*Interesting*" Catherine thought to herself quickly scribbling notes on her pad. "Please continue. Don't let my notetaking distract you."

Looking annoyed John took a deep breath before continuing. "And at one point I went to visit an attorney about seeking a divorce. Upon return from this meeting and as a visual sign of my disgust with her, I had my sons place a piece of plywood between our beds."

"That's rather dramatic but I guess it gets the point across" Catherine remarked with a shy smile on her face. But I'm not sure how you can do this with a double bed."

"Well, you can't really" John explained. "When we moved into our new home, Mercedes got rid of our queen mattress and purchased two single Tempur-Pedic® adjustable twin beds and pushed these together so that it would appear to be a double bed, when all the while it was two separate beds. This allowed enough space between the two mattresses to slide this piece of plywood right in place. When she asked about why the plywood was there, I went on a tirade while lying in bed that night. I went on to say that I did not want to see her again, hear from her again, look at her, talk with her or have anything to do with her ever again, or words to this effect. I must've fallen asleep shortly after this tirade because I'm not sure what happened after that. The next morning, I just remember that I woke up and knew it was later than what we normally slept in on Saturday. Although no clock was available, I could just tell by the light that was coming in the room from outside was more than what it would normally be. So to start the day I started calling to her to get her attention. I was unsuccessful in doing so. After a very short while my concern for her condition became elevated. I started to throw things over the plywood wall that I created in order to gain her attention, but to no avail. I could hear her breathing which did not sound normal. It sounded more like a gurgling sound. Soon my concern became borderline frantic!"

"So even though you did not want to talk to her, you still were concerned for her well-being" Catherine interjected "*interesting*" she thought to herself.

"David and Daniel were on the other side of the house. In order for me to contact them I had to call out and call out loud. This was very difficult for me because my voice is no longer as strong as it used to be and my bedroom door, as well as theirs, was closed. By time my sons arrived in the room my voice was almost gone. I told them that their mother was having some type of a medical emergency and to please call 911."

"And up until this point you had no idea what was going on" Catherine asked to reaffirm her suspicion.

"No ma'am" John said while shaking his head from side to side indicating a negative response. "By time I got to the emergency room she had been admitted into ICU and was in a coma. A deputy that was there in the room when I arrived and told me her blood culture came back positive for marijuana and asked me if I had any idea why or how this could be. At that time I explained to him that I had medication at home, prescribed by a doctor that was a marijuana derivative, but other than that I had no further explanation. The deputy informed me that they inspected that bottle and because I had several bottles of the same prescription there was no way they could tell if she used any of it or not.

The next several days seemed to be the longest time frame of our marriage. The day she went in with a coma both of my sons, their girlfriends, Tammy and I stayed in the ICU until they would throw us out around 4 o'clock in the morning. We would go home at that time and return by 8 o'clock in the morning." John stopped for a minute and looked down at his useless hands yet again. "I don't mean to sound selfish and what I'm about ready to say, but this was a very stressful time. As a patient with MS, we do not handle stress very well. My symptoms of muscle spasms really started to take hold. But be that as it may, or as the French say, Telle est la vie" John said as he allowed his voice to trail off before continuing.

Catherine, once again interrupting, said "and what does that mean?"

John responded, "such is life." Gathering his thoughts, he redirected the conversation and returned to the subject at hand, "during this time that the ICU staff would run us off, they would clean the general area and conduct a shift change. Other than that, I was there every hour. The first night I had spent by her side in the ICU holding her hand. I remember crying and saying things like please bring her back to me he can have her two days a week as long as I can have her the rest of the time, or something to that effect." John paused for a moment before continuing, "it seemed like it was about 3 o'clock in the morning and I was in the ICU, when Mercedes's brother arrived. He lives locally and just got off work."

"Does the rest of her family live locally" Catherine asked as a matter of clarification.

"Yes, most of them live in Lakeland or very close by in the surrounding area. You see Mercedes is a Lakeland native." John remarked. "As I said earlier, this is why when I retired, we moved here."

Continuing on John said, "this was the first person to arrive from her extended family."

"So even though her family lived locally, the first person to arrive from her extended family came at 3 AM" questioned Catherine. "Don't you find this a little bit odd?"

"Not if you know the extended family" John remarked before continuing.

"My brother-in-law and I were in the ICU room with Mercedes when I was handed a paper by the hospital staff suggesting that there may be a reason to 'pull the plug'. I was to read, through the paper, and sign it. I read through the document very carefully and then gave it to her brother to read as well. I remember asking him "is this what I think it is?"

I did this not because I believe he had some form of exalted or expanded knowledge of these things, but rather just to have a second set of eyes on the document. Besides, by this time I had been going at it for quite some time and I was rather tired." John took a long drink of water from his straw before continuing. "I remember asking the hospital staff if they were looking for my approval. The response that I got back appeared to be yes, or at least they were wanting my approval. My brother-in-law at that time said something to the effect of 'this seems to be a little early'. In agreement, I took the document outside and gave it to my daughter (or at least this is how I had come to view Tammy). Again, I was looking for another opinion. Tammy read through the document quickly and said something like 'we will not be signing this'. I agreed and went back in and told the ICU staff that I would not agree to this, and I was told that it was out of my hands. I did not understand this, fortunately the decision did not have to be made. Approximately an hour later the ICU staff asked all of us to leave so they could clean up and do shift change.

We all went back to the house and grabbed about an hour and a half of rest before going back the hospital. Now I want you to know" John said rocking his chair forward, "when we went back to the house we did not go very quietly. All of us were thoroughly distraught with the consideration that Mercedes may never overcome her coma. When we got back to the hospital, much to our surprise, it was just in time for Mercedes to wake up! When she saw me, she started getting hysterical and yelling "what is he doing here! He's trying to kill me" or words this effect."

"How ironic were her choice of words" Catherine interjected.

"Yes, quite, and in retrospect perhaps she knew how this entire charade was to be played out." John responded before continuing. "Physically, her statement could not be farther from the truth. Philosophically however she probably felt that my condition was "killing" her mentally to the point where her entire life had come to an end, metaphorically speaking, because I was no longer able to do those things that I used to do. But in the present contents of her remarks, there in ICU, I was absolutely floored! I did not know what to say or do. At this point in time, I was told that Mercedes had written a suicide note and her two daughters, my stepdaughter's that I had known and cared for since 1990 were now convinced that somehow I, a quadriplegic, miraculously got up in the middle of the night and wrote the suicide note that I had yet to see! I did not know what to say or do with regards to such an outlandish accusation. I was an emotional wreck!"

Shaking her head in disbelief Catherine interjected "did they honestly believe what they were saying?"

"The sad part of this is, I believe they did" John remarked as he continued. "By now other members of the family arrived at the hospital. One came as far away as Texas and even packed a black dress for her visit. It is at this point that I must remind you that although this was Mercedes's family, these are the people that I had come to know over the past 20 years or more! I thought we were on good terms, until this day. Everyone was sitting in the waiting room because only two family members at a time were allowed to go back to visit her. While everyone was waiting, family members were all talking back and forth amongst themselves totally excluding me from the conversation. Everyone was comparing their own list to see who might have Daniel's phone number. No one ever bothered to even ask, or indicate, that I may know what this number was. So, finally even though I was obviously being shunned, I spoke out in a very loud voice from my reclined power chair and said something to the effect of "gee I wonder who might possibly have Daniel's phone number?" A hush (or at least it seemed like one) fell over the room."

"I would think so" again interjected Catherine.

John continued without acknowledging her response "my brother-in-law, Bob, a rather decent guy, although he has an extreme alcoholic problem, that I had always gotten along with got up and came over and asked me if I knew Daniel's cell phone number. I said something effect of "of course!" I then gave him the number and he went back and shared it amongst all the other family members. Throughout the remainder of the day, I would repeatedly attempt to go back into the ICU to see Mercedes and twice I was ordered off the unit because I was considered a disruption."

"I would imagine that this was quite the scene" said Catherine with a slight giggle. "Do go on."

"I could just imagine the report to security" John said smiling in return. "During this time, I had come to understand that Mercedes was being detained under what Florida law considers as a Baker act. This is when individuals are not operating with what is determined by law enforcement as full mental capacity possibly present a harm to themselves or others. Once she was considered medically stable in the ICU she was taken up to the psychiatric ward of the local hospital. There she had to be evaluated by a psychiatrist before they could determine what they were to do. That night I called my mother-in-law to let her know that I would do everything I could to get Mercedes home."

This struck Catherine to be rather odd behavior considering this was his mother-in-law. So, she asked, "What prompted you to do this."

"I did this" explained John "because I knew that my mother-in-law, Haley, did not have a strong support system at home. Haley had witnessed firsthand her own brother slip in and out of variety of levels of mental health. There were other accounts that Haley's own father had been discharged from the Army in the 1950s for mental health issues. To complicate matters even more, Mercedes's father, Haley's husband was not, what I would call, a stable individual. He had a very nasty and depressing outlook on life to say the least."

"And how is that" question Catherine.

"Probably the best way to describe it is the way Mercedes would describe it."

"And how was that" Catherine questioned inquisitively.

"She used to say that her father had many demons that would cause him to act out, let's just say in a manner that is not socially acceptable."

"How would that be" question Catherine for now for curiosity was truly aroused.

"Mind you I have never seen any of this" recanted John, "I only see the aftereffects."

"And what would those be" again questioned Catherine, rather forcibly this time in order to continue the conversation.

"Well, there were things like a pair of vise grips stabbed into a banana, or paint thrown on the wall"

"Paint on the wall surely doesn't sound like an act of hysteria" interrupted Catherine.

"True, true" John said as he nodded his head in agreement, "but it was applied more with the bucket!"

"What you mean" question Catherine rather inquisitively all the while leaving open a very large question.

"I mean" clarified John "that it looked like somebody just took a bucket of paint and threw it up against the wall. But that wasn't the half of it" explain John. "My favorite was the electrical wires pulled out of the wall."

Showing a little bit more excitement, Catherine interjected "well this I know something about. My husband has been rewiring some rental property we own, and I have been helping him" Catherine responded with a somewhat level of confidence. "But do go on."

"So, you're familiar with the large electrical cable or wire that runs behind the wall" John paused, rather than to agree on common terminology. "Well, that big cable or wire was pulled out of where the light switch would have been and ripped through the drywall all the way down to the floor!"

"Still and even with all this I find this to be a very strange thing for her to say, especially about her own father" Catherine said while looking up towards John rather than in her normal fashion, which was to ask him questions while still looking at her notepad, and never looking back up. "I mean to say I do not have a strong background in all of that, but it is an interesting comment to make especially of one's own father."

"You did not know her father" John said with a sly smile before continuing. "But it was because of these issues and much more that I wanted to assure her (Haley) that I would not let her daughter suffer a similar fate as her brother did. She thanked me for the phone conversation. The next day, true to my word, I told the psychiatrist that she, Mercedes, was okay to come home. In retrospect I wonder if this was the best decision." John said, again drifting off before continuing. "The next several days at home were very troublesome but at the same time it was calming because I did not hear anything about her boyfriend or wanting to go visit him. So, I was hoping that whatever she went through while in the hospital changed her mind and she would give up on pursuing this individual."

"Why were these next few days troubling for you, John" Catherine said leaning forward in such manner as to place her elbows on her knees.

"You know just plain asking that question it would appear to me that you don't really pay attention. If she is released home, that's my home and I'm not able to do anything without assistance. If I am confined in a room with someone who is not in charge of all of their faculties, it could become very interesting very quickly."

"I wonder what type of individual actually goes through all this" Catherine began to wonder to herself.

Oblivious to Catherine's private questions, John continued to unveil his story. "Approximately two or three weeks went by, and she started taking up with her boyfriend again telling me that he wanted her to move in with him and that he loved her. At the same time, she developed a habit of getting real close to me and yelling things such as "you're not a man! If you are a real man, you would have killed yourself already. You're dead, you're dead already!" This would generally be followed by hitting me on the shoulder or the side of the arm. I had extreme difficulty with grasping this entire concept, the concept of her behavior and dealing with my own deteriorating body. Shortly before Halloween I was at a real low point and honestly and sincerely was at or pretty near wits end and seriously contemplated suicide."

"Suicide" Catherine almost screamed all the while looking rather panicked.

"Relax," John reassured her. "Caution interceded because somewhere I thought the Bible said it is the unforgivable sin if one commits suicide. Death by suicide, I thought, would certainly condemn one to hell! I asked several friends if they agreed with my assumption. Everyone said that they believed that was just a Catholic belief and it did not say that in the Bible. So, I did something that I should've done years ago, I prayed."

"Interesting" Catherine said while holding her pencil up to her mouth. "You don't strike me as a very religious person so why did you settle on this course of action" questioned Catherine.

"Well, you see my grandfather was a servant of the Lord" John explained "and he became one after he had prayed for God to preserve his life when he became deathly ill in 1919. When I prayed, I too made this vow that if God could save me from this torment, I would be his servant for the rest of my life."

"And are you, I mean are you a servant of Jesus Christ" questioned Catherine.

This question took John rather by surprise. Since this whole ordeal started no one questioned his level of loyalty or religious frame of reference. So, John responded the only way he knew how by saying "I am doing my best every day to put the Lord first in my life and above all else. As a matter fact I now consider myself to be a child of God as it states in the book of Romans." John responded while looking directly into Catherine's eyes "and I'm proud to say it."

"*So convenient for these types of people to speak to God*" Catherine thought to herself quietly. Interjecting once again Catherine said, "please go on and tell me more."

Taking a sip of something to drink John began again. "Approximately one month went past and I had a dream. This was rather unusual, as I had not had a dream since high school. At any rate, in this dream I was presented with pictures of long-time friends parting ways. As a backdrop to this there was an overwhelming voice. The voice was very strong yet loving. You could tell it was from an older man, but you could not tell from which direction the voice was coming from. The voice was very soothing and was coming from everywhere! My first inclination was that it was God. Then I remembered asking myself "why would God talk to me?" This was immediately followed by "who am I to question God." Then I started to think that this voice may be of the Devil. That was immediately set aside because the voice was too kind."

"What was the voice saying" blurted out Catherine.

"The voice just kept saying over and over 'it will be okay; it will be okay'. I pondered this for many days. At first, I did not want to believe it and just continue on with my plans of suicide. I had these plans fine-tuned to the point where I knew the only way for me to kill myself was if I threw myself into the pool. I then realized that there were several obstacles to overcome with this idea."

"Such as?" Catherine asked while tapping her pencil against her cheek.

"First," John began, "I needed to be seat belted into my chair, otherwise I would just float to the top. Secondly, the water had to be warm otherwise cold water would just preserve my body making a successful rescue more probable. The final problem was I had to make sure that my boys were not around and that I had a caregiver, who, in my opinion would have too much difficulty in rescuing me."

"It seems like you had this well planned out" Catherine once again interjected. "If you had carried out your plans and committed suicide while a caregiver, innocent enough, was there to take care of you, you realize what this would have done to their mindset" Catherine questioned. "I mean it is horrible enough as it would be for you to take your own life, but in doing so must you destroy the life of another innocent person?"

John looked back up at Catherine with a rather blank face. "No; that thought never even crossed my mind" John explained. "I would not want to do that besides by December of the same year I got a urinary tract infection (UTI) and she, Mercedes, took me to the VA hospital in Tampa. She was anxious for me to stay over the Christmas period but I was released one or two days before Christmas. This was Christmas 2014 our last Christmas together. I remember she bought me a book on a disk so that I could read the book while at my computer. At the same time, she bought her boyfriend a $300 pair of binoculars. New Year's Eve was spent sitting in my bedroom with the door closed because I was infuriated by what my wife was saying. We had gotten into an argument earlier that evening when she started saying next New Year's Eve she was going to go out and leave me home. I went into the bedroom and closed the door, so I did not have to hear about it. Several hours went by and I felt or rather *sensed* that she was scratching at the door. I tried to open the door but despite my efforts I could not. So, in my drunken stupor I drove my chair through the closed bedroom door! Well, of course I only made it halfway through the door until my forward movement came to a halt."

"And why was that" questioned Catherine.

"I guess my chair lacked the necessary power to continue all the way through. At any rate, my wife and stepdaughter came over and told me because I was so stupid to do this to myself, I would just have to sit there till morning!"

"So, she just felt comfortable leaving you there" questioned Catherine.

"Yeah, pretty much" John nodded before continuing. "You see in retrospect I believe that there were demons at play here and possibly that was what was scratching at the door" John said with a very serious look on his face. Up until this point John looked much like any other person except a level of seriousness was not present on his face. He seemed to be a very happy-go-lucky type of person, up until this point. "My son Daniel came home from his date probably around two or three in the morning and got me out of the door. Throughout the remaining year of 2015 my wife would constantly get in my face and scream "you're dead, you're dead! Don't you get it, you're dead! You can't do anything!" She would tell me other things such as "you're not a real man. Real men that I know would have killed themselves years ago rather than putting their family through all this. You should have been a real man like Robin Williams, but no you are a selfish Bastard!"

"This is horrible" Catherine interjected. "Well," she questioned, do you think that you were acting selfish? Or do you just believe it was almost as if she was trying to push you over the edge, so to speak."

"On this particular occasion, I don't think I was selfish at all, but I think it was more the latter. Yes, she had me pretty much 'on the ropes' John agreed as he continued. "Time went on you see and I just kept thinking of what God had said 'it will be okay'. I kept thinking of this over and over and relying on it to settle my very soul. Easter of 2015 my loving wife and stepdaughter went to Easter dinner without me and left me at home for about six hours."

"Where did they go" asked Catherine.

"They went to St. Petersburg" John responded with a nod. "By time they got back, I was having a severe asthma attack, yet my wife would not give me my breather until late in the evening. By this time, I had been stressed for approximately eight hours! She also refused to get me out of my chair so that I could get into bed and sleep peacefully. This was probably one of my worst nights."

"I would say so" Catherine interjected in agreement. "Please go on. I will try to limit my interjections to allow you to finish."

John nodded and continued with his sordid tale "Unbeknownst to me at the time, it was sometime during the spring that Mercedes had cashed in her IRA, which was solely compiled during our marriage, and purchased a 37 ½ foot boat with twin inboard engines. The boat itself cost $80,000 with a $7500 down payment! Her name was the only one on the title but looking through the purchase documents her boyfriend was apparently posing as her husband all throughout this transaction. I later found out that she was to put her boyfriend on the title to the boat but was unable to because they were not married.

Shortly after Easter, yet before summer, Mercedes had what, I can best describe as another episode. It was sometime in May and the VA had given me an emergency call button to wear around my neck. This was one of those buttons where if I had a problem, I could push it and be connected with somebody who could assist or activate the 911 system. I would have one of the caregivers put the button around my neck every night when they put me into bed. On one occasion I remember sitting up in bed watching TV minding my own business. Mercedes was home and was occupied with something somewhere in the house. It was after dark so that must've been somewhere after 9 o'clock pm. I cannot remember exactly what led up to this, but I remember Mercedes coming into the bedroom wrapped in a beach towel and yelling at me while waving a steak knife that she had obtained from the kitchen. She said that she was going to kill herself by throwing herself in the swimming pool and slicing her wrists. I just remember her yelling something to the effect and that I could not do anything about it and then in the morning I would just see her dead corpse floating in the pool. I then heard the door onto the lanai open and something enter the pool! I was frantic! I could not get up and I could not call anyone except using my button on my alert system. So, this is what I did. For an emergency alert button, it proved to be quite challenging. Even with this around my neck I had a hard time accessing and pressing down the button. You see my fingers were failing and the added stress did not help."

"I'm sure it didn't" reassured Catherine. "Stress, mental and/or physical can be somewhat of an analogous to what kryptonite is for Superman for an MS patient."

"Well, I can tell you it wasn't doing me any good" John explained. "And that's a good analogy by the way."

"What is that" Catherine asked.

"The kryptonite to Superman as is stress is to an MS patient" John said before taking another drink water. "I'm sorry to be drinking so much water but my medications cause horrific dry mouth" John explained. Continuing on, John said "I wrather considered a form of atonement"

Again, very interesting pillow "No bother" Catherine said out of surprise. "*Interesting*" Catherine thought to herself before waving her hand to move the conversation along.

"Shortly after she left the room I heard one set of our lanai doors open and the little alarm that alerts me whenever an exterior door is opened, went "beep, beep." This was shortly followed by the sound of something getting into the pool. I was frantic! I don't mind telling you. I could not move and even if I was able to, I might have been immobilized by fear. This is how bad it was for me. I was mortified and to top it all off my stupid fingers could not push the button on the emergency alert button."

"And why do you think that was" questioned Catherine.

"My MS prohibits me from the manipulation of my fingers." John explained in a rather haughty tone as if he expected the social worker to already understand this. "*She probably already does and is so burnt out that she just does not care anymore*" John thought to himself before continuing. "The only way I was able to activate the alarm was by first getting the cord in my mouth and then working it slowly until I could get the alarm button itself into my mouth. At that point it took me a few trials and errors before I was able to bite it."

"What happens when you push the button" Catherine asked. "I mean do you hear other people on the other end?"

"I did not know what to expect" explained John, who was at the time was struggling to suppress an ever-present level of emotion. "I mean I had never used one before. It was my only hope." John just kind of leaned his head back as if to present his face to the sky, however his headrest presented him from doing so. After holding his head in that manner for a few seconds as if he was reminiscing, he continued. "You see by design it will ring four numbers before it automatically calls 911.

We had it set up to call Mercedes's phone first, then to my son David (his twin brother was over in Virginia) then to his twin brother Daniel and finally to a friend of mine down the road. Well on that night calling Mercedes would not have been a brilliant idea." John said with a smile. "So, it next went to David. Well, he had just changed his phone number and I did not have time to upload it into the system so that would not work either. Finally, it went to my son who was in Virginia. And this is where the record gets blurred" John explained. "You see both my son who was in Virginia and my friend who was down the street both claim that they got the message that night. So, whoever it was, "they" are the ones that called 911.

By the time the police arrived, she got up out of the pool and was dripping wet and denying everything. After the police took my statement, and took hers, once again she was Baker Acted and taken into custody. Sometime before the sun came up, Mercedes was released into the custody of her younger son who was also a sheriff's deputy. On this particular morning, my caregiver came in and got me up, as she did every morning. As part of this process, every morning when I go to leave my bedroom, I have to roll out onto the lanai in order to get to the main part of the house. This is because my bedroom doorway is too narrow for my chair and it's physically impossible to make it large enough to accommodate my chair. So, I go across the pool deck, no biggie" John said, again with a smile. "When I went by the pool on this particular morning, I saw the steak knife on the bottom. By time I got in the kitchen Mercedes was at the counter, fuming. She ordered the caregiver out of the house, ripped off my emergency call button, ripped the device out of the wall in the bedroom and threw it all away! It took me several hours to get her to calm down."

"You mean to tell me that an individual who is just spent the night in police custody under the auspices of the Baker Act is now home alone with you, a quadriplegic," said Catherine astonishingly. "Unbelievable" she said shaking her head. "Do, please go on."

"It was rather touch and go there for a while, but I eventually got her to calm down. In doing so, I also got her to remove the steak knife from the pool. If the deputies knew how to turn pool lights on, they would've seen the steak knife on the bottom of the pool. Once again, in retrospect maybe they should've seen it.

At this point it must be understood that throughout most of 2015, when Mercedes was home, which was most of the time, even if it was only three or four days a week, I was in constant mental torment."

"*That's an understatement*" Catherine thought to herself.

Once again oblivious to what Catherine was thinking about, John just continued or at this point he was truly on a roll! "If I had asked for something such as mouthwash or lip balm Mercedes would generally respond with something like "you don't need that! No one's kissing you." She would also say things such as "I just can't take you anywhere" or "I'm tired of having to make special arrangements to take you somewhere" or words to this effect."

"I'm sorry" Catherine interjected. "I can't sit here quietly anymore. It's as if she was wanting to push you over the edge or perhaps, she was actually having a mental breakdown herself."

"I thought about this" John explained before continuing "it also must be understood that during this time Mercedes went out and got a facelift, hair extensions and fake eyelashes. Oh, and these were not the cheap ones either" explained John. "These were the horsehair eyelashes and cost well over $100 and last for about three weeks. During this period one of her more favorite lines or more correctly, reoccurring themes, was "if you are a real man, you would kill yourself." When she found out that when I had my pulmonary embolism in 2013 that the emergency room doctor said something to the effect of that I could walk out of the emergency room and would probably be dead in an hour, Mercedes was livid! She screamed at me on numerous occasions telling me that I was selfish and that I should have just gone ahead and walked out and died that way I would not have to put my family through everything that I had.

End of June beginning of July 2015 my wife put me into the VA hospital for a two-week period so that she could go on vacation with her boyfriend. She was very excited to go on this vacation and decided to tell me that they were going to a special place her boyfriend told her about. This special place was only accessible by water! It was called Cabbage Key, as if this had some significance to it. During my stay at the VA was the first time that I mentioned her boyfriend's existence to the social worker at the VA. Although the social worker was somewhat understanding, the psychiatrist she sent me to was not helpful at all. I was having extreme difficulty in sleeping, often waking up at 3 o'clock in the morning and just lying there all night. To remedy this my doctor even gave me another pill purposely designed to let me sleep through the night because I was so disturbed by what she (Mercedes) was doing. When she came back from vacation, she seemed to be excited about explaining, in detail, all of her exploits often emphasizing any sexual experiences that she might've had. At the same time, she told me a story that I can only describe as unsubstantiated. She said that when she was on vacation with her boyfriend, she jumped overboard into the Gulf! Again, I feel compelled to reiterate the fact that this is now considered hearsay because this part of my story as unsubstantiated. Having said that again, Mercedes told me that she jumped into the Gulf with the intent on killing herself. The story that she told me seemed to be very similar to a story from her adolescent years. She told me years ago that when she was a teenager, she had severe bouts of depression. On one such occasion she had jumped into the water and started swimming out to sea because she no longer wanted to live. Another cheerleading friend of hers, I believe her name was Melanie, called to her and started wadding out into the water. Mercedes used to say that this was the only reason why she turned around and came back to the shore because she knew her friend, Maria, could not swim. At any rate, I digress. She said it took her boyfriend and another boater over an hour to get her back onboard. I asked her at the time if the Coast Guard was notified or the local police or medical authority. She told me no, no one was contacted so I have no actual record of this other than what she told me.

August of the same year marked our 25th wedding anniversary. A milestone to some. That morning I woke up when the caregiver rang the doorbell. As soon as Mercedes got up to answer the door she went straight to the back room where the computer was kept. Throughout our entire marriage we could not wait to "see" who would be the first one to say, "happy birthday" or "happy Father's Day" or "happy Mother's Day." Mercedes said none of this to me when she got up. As the caregiver was getting me ready to get up, I felt like I was going to throw up so I asked for a bucket. After spitting-up a little, I sent the caregiver back to ask my wife what she wanted to do for the day. When the caregiver came back and told me that my wife was arguing with some man on the phone. I knew what she was doing!

It was shortly after this, in a fleeting moment of desperation, I felt one of the best things I could say was that I wanted to go to a nursing home. Now mind you, I did not really want to go, but I rather wanted the reassurance that Mercedes would keep me around."

"You are probably saying this out of desperation" Catherine interjected.

"You're definitely right about that" John reassured her. "So, as part of this process Mercedes and I started investigating the possibility of going to a VA nursing home. There was one about an hour and ½ away from where we lived and the administrator virtual told us that they could take me almost immediately. We both went there on a tour. In doing so, when we left, we both ended up looking at each other and almost in unison saying "well that was depressing" or words to that effect. I was left with the impression that we both felt that it was way too depressing to be in a nursing home to start with and that home in particular! She, Mercedes, reinforced this thought by insisting that she would never put me in there, such a comforting thought.

By the end of September, however, she told me she had just turned the paperwork for me to go to that very nursing home that we had visited! I was absolutely livid! I refuse to go and she told me "well that is just tough because I have your Power of Attorney and I'm going to commit you." I responded by saying not if I disagree. This was early in the evening. At approximately 3 o'clock in the morning this all changed. Mercedes woke me up by yelling and screaming at me and then placed a pillow over my face."

"Are you serious" exclaimed Catherine with eyes wide open.

"I am definitely serious" John said as he turned and looked directly at her.

For the rest of his tale Catherine allowed him to continue without interruption.

"Almost instinctively, I turned my face all the way to the left. The pillow was rather substantial, a Tempur-Pedic® pillow so it could not bend easy enough for her to get a good seal. It was only because of this that I was able to survive. Then something caused her to back off. Call it something Divine... I asked her, "Are you trying to kill me?" Now it is at this point I must remind you that I'm fully aware that individuals might be somewhat foggy in their recollection of events shortly after waking but trust me by this time I was fully awake! Although the lights were rather low in the room, I can vividly recall her face. She had a very frenzied look about her when she responded, "that's the point, asshole!" She then came after me again. It was at this point that I knew she would succeed. There was nothing in her way. I put up my only working arm as a meager form of defense. She quickly brushed this aside and push down hard. Once again, I turned to the left in an attempt to breathe. She was bearing down hard, and I was soon losing the ability to breathe. Just as I thought it was all over, I heard a shuffling at the door as if somebody was struggling to get in. The door opened at about the same point that the pillow was released I saw a bright light and I thought to myself it must be true, there is a bright light in the end. I guess she was successful. The overhead lights were then flipped on, and I realized the bright light that I saw was the flashlight app on my son Daniel's phone. They, Mercedes and Daniel, started yelling back and forth. Mercedes stormed out of the room, and I told Daniel that she tried to kill me. He decided to lay down in her bed next to me. I'm not sure why he did not call 911 at this point. Perhaps he was used to the fact that we were always fighting or perhaps he did not take me seriously."

John's voice rather trailed off at this point before continuing.

"A few minutes went past and she, Mercedes, stormed back into the room yelling and screaming at my son. She told him to get out of the room, but I pleaded with him to stay. He slept on the floor at the foot of my bed for the rest of the night. When my caregiver came in the following morning, I told her all about this. She asked at that time if I wanted her to call 911 and I remembered saying no, not yet."

"Now wait a minute" interjected Catherine. "This woman just tried to kill you and you don't want anybody to call 911" questioned Catherine. "That sounds a little strange."

"Well,," John began before taking a long sip on his straw "strange as it was, I wanted to talk to Daniel in order to verify my facts. The last thing I wanted to do was say that somebody was trying to murder me, especially my wife, who I am relying upon for virtually everything! Little did I know at the time that this would be my very down fall."

"How so" Catherine asked as she leaned forward and poured herself another glass of water. All the while thinking to herself "*strange I normally keep this here for the patients. With this one being a quadriplegic, I'm the one drinking it.*"

"Well, you see" John said as he cleared his throat, "I was unwilling to call this in to make sure it just was not a bad dream. We're talking about my wife. A woman who I had known for over 25 years. I was having a real hard time wrapping my head around all this."

"Well, I guess that's understandable given the amount of drugs that you take" Catherine said.

"That and for the fact that I had just woken up" John said before continuing with his story. "Approximately 30 hours passed before I was able to discuss this with both of my sons and my daughter-in-law. I waited this long simply because I did not really feel safe in presenting it at any other time. The other aspect is I also had to wrap my head around the facts before I could make some sense of it well enough to explain it to anyone else. I started out presenting my case almost like a multiple-choice question."

"*That is not the way I would present it*" Catherine said to herself before saying "continue."

"I've been a part-time or "adjunct" instructor for college since 1987 and I guess that format was now more familiar with me. I remember choice A was commit suicide (I was still not taking this off the table)."

It was at this point that the mood in the room changed dramatically. Catherine leaned forward very quickly and placed her hand on John's leg. "Are you feeling this way now" she questioned. "If so, I can get you the help that you need, no problem."

Shaking his head from side-to-side John reassured her "oh no I don't feel like that at all now. As a matter fact I am quite the opposite, I feel at peace, an overwhelming peace!"

"Well, that's interesting, did you see another therapist" questioned Catherine as she retracted her hand. At the same time, she was asking very inquisitively because there were no notes to indicate that John had done so. "*If nothing else, you need to make sure this record reflects the truth*" Catherine thought to herself.

"No, I didn't see the need for one. I found the Lord! That's all I need. As a matter fact, that's all I ever needed. As a matter of fact ever accepting the Lord in my life, He has saved me on three separate occasions." John said before taking another long draw on his straw. "So, I knoq that My Father has something in store for me. I just have to figure out what that is. Besides, I'm only seeing you because I have to for my annual evaluation" John explained before continuing. "The next choice I had listed in my mental notes was to divorce my wife and then go to a nursing home. My third choice was to go to a nursing home and then divorce her so she would have to do all the work clearing out the house. Finally, the last choice was to do nothing at all because I was still relying on what God said to me in that "*It would be okay.*" After all, relying on this and repeating it almost as a mantra for the past several months was how I survived up until this point."

"So, what did you settle on or is this when God stepped in" Catherine interjected, at this point she was just dying to know how someone can go from the point of such dire desperation to feeling at peace. "*Maybe he was just using all this as a metaphor*" Catherine began to think herself

"True to form my decision was made for me, yes, God stepped in, and in a big way!" John explained. "My sons would not let me finish my story and kept cutting me off before I could get to the other choices on my list. All they ever really heard was my first choice that is committing suicide. Both David and his wife, Naomi insisted that they had a duty of first report. They argued with me that their careers were just starting their career and that they could not let this issue go. You see, David had just become a sheriff's deputy and Naomi had just become a registered nurse. So, not bothering to hear me out, David went into another room and called the report in. With the act of calling this in, somehow this got recorded as Daniel reporting it rather than David. As expected, the deputies came out to the house to take the report. One Deputy pressured me until well after midnight to tell him my side of the story. Despite his best attempts I refused by simply telling him "I know what you want me to say but I do not want the mother of my children sent to jail."

"So, even when you had your opportunity you still would not report her or am I missing something" interjected Catherine.

"Yeah, pretty much" explain John. "You see, once again I had not had the opportunity to discuss with Daniel to find out what he remembered from that night. As such, I was unwilling to make any false statements against anyone." John said before adjusting his legs yet once again. "You see, I have somewhat of limited knowledge when it comes to these matters, and I want to make sure that I was doing the right thing. At any rate, I had sufficiently worn down the Deputy to the point that he told me "Well I have enough from your sons to swear out a warrant anyway even without your statement." With that, the deputy left our house, and I was finally able to get some sleep. I guess David waited about a day before he decided to notify his stepsister, Tammy, of the impending arrest warrant. I'm not sure if David knew it or not that at the time Tammy was with her mother at Universal Studios Halloween Horror Nights. Before turning herself in on Sunday, October 4 Mercedes withdrew $600 from our joint checking account for some unknown reason. She turned herself in in the late afternoon. I actually drove down to the county jail just to see if there was anything I could do. In which case there was absolutely nothing I could do, and I was not even able to talk with anyone. In retrospect this was a rather stupid thing for me to do, anyway."

"Why do you think this was stupid" questioned Catherine as a way of possibly delving into his inner thoughts. "I mean I don't have any experience in these matters, but it would seem to me to be a very logical thing to do especially if you're truly in love with the person, as you so state."

"I don't know what I was thinking at the time." John said with a rather blank look on his face. "All I know is my wife of 25 years, my little baby, was being arrested on something that I had said. I had the worst feeling in my stomach possibly the worst a person could have. I felt I had betrayed my one true love, even though I knew it in my heart that she tried to kill me. I guess the true reality of it all had not quite set in. The next day was the day of Mercedes's first report. This meant she was brought before a judge via video camera and the judge would determine if she would be bonded out. At that hearing, family members were unable to interject or say anything. David and his wife actually went and sat at the jail so as to be there for Mercedes while Daniel came with me to the courthouse. Her bond was denied, thank the Lord!

Daniel took me out to the car. You see I say this because although I had the ability to drive my power chair with my one good hand, I was so emotionally strained that I was unable to do so. By time we arrived at the car, Daniel received a text message from the Deputy that had come out to the house as part of the investigation and the same one that wanted my statement. The Deputy was at the courthouse and agreed to meet us at the car. He, the Deputy, showed me two different sworn statements that Mercedes had made to two different Deputies when she was arrested. Both statements were almost identical copies of each other. I had to read them both at least five times each until it sunk in. I kept reading her statement over and over in total disbelief. She talked about how she realized that she could be stuck with me for the next 14 years or so and she did not want to do that. Beyond the obvious, the statement that she made that really stayed with me was "I just wanted to be with my friends (meaning her boyfriend and his two teenage daughters) and my grandbabies. That's why I did it." I remember reading this over and over and then looking up at Daniel and the Deputy and saying, "correct me if I am wrong but did, she just confess?" Both Daniel and the Deputy said almost in unison "sure sounds like a confession to me" or words to that effect. What baffled me by this statement more than anything else was that she did not include her own children or her siblings, just her boyfriend and grandbabies. Even now as I'm writing this more than a year and a half later, I still find it hard to believe."

"I would say so" Catherine interjected. "I know, I know" Catherine said as she was waving her hand "I said I would not interject, and I did. Please, continue."

"The next day my biggest task became taking hold of my finances" John said.

"The next day" Catherine once again interjected this time with a certain level of excitement. "I would've thought this was something that you would do rather immediately."

"Well," John began rather methodically, "she was arrested on a Sunday afternoon. The next morning, she was arraigned before the magistrate. Then I had my little discussion with the Deputy. By time I returned home the reporters were there. So, this had been a little time-consuming" John explained.

"To complicate matters even further" John continued, "up until this point Mercedes had exclusive access to all financial matters, family email accounts and passwords. Despite repeated requests for her to share these with me, she refused and constantly changed both username and passwords. For some reason the first account I went to tackle was my USAA savings account. This account was supposed to hold my earnings from two different colleges that I was teaching at. I had instructed Mercedes to send whatever money I generated from these two different colleges into this account so that it would not be scarfed up into our family budget but held in reserve as a savings. Something told me that this had not been done so it was not overly surprising when I saw it only held close to $800."

"It seems like you are expecting this" Catherine interjected.

"I had suspicions let's just say" John continued. "Borrowing money from Daniel, I hired the same attorney that I had spoken to in September 2014. I wanted this individual to swear out a permanent restraining order against Mercedes and file for divorce. Daniel wrote out the check and presented this to the attorney. After speaking to USAA, I removed Mercedes from my car insurance and bank account. Next, I called on a local friend of mine and told him about my dilemma, he suggested that his wife go by to help me because she was really good at searching through records. His wife, Janet came by and through a series of phone calls and emails she quickly identified what credit cards were open and to what extent the balances were. I called in all the credit cards as being lost because I did not know where these were, and some had a good deal of money available for use on them. The next day, we went to my local servicing bank. When I introduced myself and told the bank representative who I was, they all knew of the story because the local news stations (ABC, CBS, Fox News, NBC and a local cable company) had all ran the story. The individuals at the bank where more than happy to help."

"*Sounds to me more like grandstanding*" Catherine said to herself.

"It was shortly after this that Daniel was notified by the attorney's office that his check somehow bounced and was returned from his bank.

He immediately checked his funds and somehow $3500 was removed from his account the day after his mother was arrested! I remember at the time the Deputy investigating the case and who had eventually taken my statement, told me they had recordings from the phone in the jail where Mercedes had been sharing what he called financial information with someone over the phone. I can only guess this was to access money in Daniel's account as well as to shift other assets around. Once again, I was floored with the fact that his mother stole money from him!"

"So" questioned Catherine as she was attempting to clarify his statements. "After all that had been said and done by this woman, you are questioning her ability to take money from her son."

"Well, yes, yes I was" John stated. "You see I may be a lot of things" John explained, "I have never and would never steal from my own children! After all, this was her child as well as mine. I swore to him right then "Daniel, I don't know how, and I don't know when, but this will be the first account that I pay back. But I will make you whole.""

"How were you going to do this" questioned Catherine.

"Wasn't really sure of the time" John said. "During this time, I just started praying every night and every morning. I kept asking God for help and assistance in understanding why this happened and how I could possibly begin to wrap my arms around the problem. At the same time, I also prayed to comfort and care for Mercedes as well as all those who loved and cared for her, including her boyfriend! This last one was a real struggle for me as it remains today. However, I did it as I felt I needed to do."

"*Another interesting choice of words*" Catherine thought to herself all the while presenting the question, "why did you feel it necessary to pray for her and her boyfriend?"

"The Bible tells us that if we judge other people, we will be judged by the same standard" John said while looking straight at Catherine.

Catherine just looked at John while the next question formulated in her head. "*I have heard of individuals becoming religious under stressful situations, so is this going to be one of those stories*" Catherine thought to herself before allowing him to continue.

"Within a week all the credit cards that I called in as lost started having replacement cards arrive in the mail" John explained. "One card in particular that had a considerable amount of money still on it and in my wife's name, came with a stack of checks. As an authorized user on this account, I was able to pay Daniel off in full. My prayer was answered!

Slowly but surely the financial web of intrigue woven by my wife was peeled back layer by layer. At one point in time, prior to all of this happening, Mercedes and I were talking about purchasing an RV large enough to accommodate my handicap needs. This would include an overhead hoist to get me from my chair into my bed, a therapeutic bed and a ramp so that I could get in and out. All this was considered possible. Considering my penchant for camping, and my limitations in traveling this was considered to be the ultimate answer so that I could continue to enjoy and participate in family events like an upcoming family reunion in Vancouver. I suggested that we go to a local RV dealer that had a test drive track so that Mercedes could see if she was able to drive the RV. Several days passed and then she suggested that instead of her driving the RV that we hire somebody to drive it for us. I asked her who she had in mind and then she revealed to me that she wanted her boyfriend to drive us to my family reunion!"

"How did this make you feel" Catherine asked inquisitively and then realizing the stupidity of her question after it left her lips.

"Well, I was absolutely appalled at the idea and rejected it immediately" John said abruptly! "After that, all talk of purchasing an RV went away. It was only after I assumed control of the family finances that I found out why. All spring and summer long prior to Mercedes's attempt on my life, she had been talking about going out on her boyfriend's boat. As I was digging through the financial mess that I was left to deal with, it became clear to me that Mercedes had cashed in her IRA and purchased a 37 ½ foot yacht that was docked in St. Petersburg, Florida which was about 50 miles away. Unfortunately for me, when I called the marina the marina manager informed me that they did not have any record of insurance on this yacht and the slip rental was $650 per month and it was already two months in arrears. Further, I had to make sure that electricity was run to the boat to keep the electric bilge pump powered and I had to provide proof of insurance. So, on top of everything else, I now had to provide insurance for a boat that I had never seen, provide electricity to the same boat and pay the slip rental!

In total, I found at least 14 credit cards, most of which were charged up totally. On top of this I had life insurance to the amount of $1.4 million on me, most of which was owned solely by Mercedes which meant I could not change the beneficiary. So, most of these I had let go simply because I wanted to control my own destiny. One bill that kept coming back on numerous occasions was for medical procedures that Mercedes had in 2015. These included the facelift that I asked how this was going to be paid for and she informed me that she was going to borrow money on her IRA, a breast enlargement procedure and a breast lift procedure. These last two procedures had to be accomplished in Fort Lauderdale, Florida, approximately six hours away from where I live. When I asked her how she was getting down there, she informed me that her boyfriend would drive the Cadillac down there with her in it. This is the very same car that I purchased off the showroom floor in 2010 as our 20th anniversary gift. It cost me $900 per month for five years! Now she was letting her boyfriend drive it everywhere! This was obviously a bill that I was not going to pay. All throughout the early months of her incarceration, I was told by two different detectives and the state attorney who is handling the case, that there were recordings over the phone in the jail where Mercedes had been sharing financial information with somebody else on the phone."

"Who do you suppose she was talking with" Catherine asked.

"I'm not really sure. If I were to wager a guess," John said. "My guess would be either my stepdaughter who is an accountant with the FBI or her boyfriend."

"I mean" Catherine said, "was she always like this? Or more directly, did she always act in this manner, or did she change?"

John once again shifted in his chair utilizing mechanical support system activated through the joystick up to his chin. "You see my wife went to her 40th high school reunion in June of 2014. She decided that she did not want to take me because I was in a power chair. So she went with her daughter, my stepdaughter that I raised since she was approximately five. From what Mercedes told me, she was sitting there watching everyone having fun with their significant others, some of these people were individuals that Mercedes had despised even back in high school. Now, without confirming this for a second time with

Mercedes, let me elaborate. There were several individuals in her high school that she did not like. These were the same individuals that were, again according to Mercedes, now out enjoying retired life together with their significant others. On many occasions, there were even video clips being played at the reunion of these very same people out enjoying life. This was something that Mercedes mentioned to me some time later that we would never be able to do. I remember vividly sitting on my back lanai overlooking the golf course and seeing a group of golfers that were approximately at our age. Mercedes turned to me and said something to the effect of "see that? That is something we will never have, just enjoying the afternoon together." In retrospect I believe she was saying these things to help justify any actions that she may have been contemplating. As mentioned previously, it was sometime later, perhaps near the end of July, that she asked me something to the effect of her wanting to have sex again. She was asking me, or at least justifying her already made decision by asking for permission to have an affair. I remember thinking about this for quite some time in responding "as long as it is only once a month and I don't know anything about it, I would be fine with that." She took this as her license to do with as she will! This concept of me not knowing quickly went by the wayside as well as the once-a-month idea! Both of these suggestions very quickly turned into once a week, twice a week and then ultimately up to four times a week. It was jealousy on Mercedes's part. She was so jealous of her former high school classmates that she had to outperform in some form or fashion. Once her need for jealousy was fulfilled by having a boyfriend, buying a yacht, and all of her other extreme expenses, her need for fulfillment turned more toward greed. The only way to sustain such an expensive lifestyle as the one that she had built was to constantly find more money in which to spend. To satisfy the need for jealousy is much like filling the need of a crack addict. Money, and lots of it, are needed to sustain such a need. The night in question we had been arguing. This was the fact that totally escaped me until recently."

"And what point was that" Catherine asked.

"The fact that we had been arguing" John said. "I guess I was so wrapped up with trying to remember what happened to me that I forgot to remember what happened prior.

That evening, the night in question," John added for clarification "when she tried to murder me, Mercedes informed me that she had just filled out the paperwork and sent them off to commit me to a nursing home. I told her that I was not going. That is when the argument ensued. She yelled at me something to the effect that I was going and that I could not do anything about it because she had my Power of Attorney. I informed her that might be true but if I object to it, I could not be committed. I had this fact verified when I visited the very nursing home that we agreed was too horrible for me to go to, yet it was the very one that she wanted to pack me off to! We argue back and forth for some time until I must've drifted off to sleep. As she did so often, after I was asleep, she must've continued to drink. The vision now is very clear in my mind. She must have sat there and drank an untold number of cocktails of Bacardi® light rum with Diet Coke® at a 50-50 mix. I'm sure she sat there in deep concentration staring at the TV. It would not have mattered if the TV was on or off. I know my words were resonating in her mind. This was the opportunity that Satan had been waiting! Then he started his snake-like tongue saying things, I guess, that would get her to start thinking. *Why should I have all this money? Why could she not enjoy life? Why could she not have fun? After all, I'm the one in a power chair. It was my life that was over not hers. Certainly, why I don't want her to have fun?"*

It was these words or something to this effect that kept rolling around in her mind over and over and over. It was Satan's way of working his will. This, I believe, is what drove her to attempt to kill me that night. If she had been successful, she must've rationalized, that she would receive approximately $1.4 million in life insurance. This would be enough to sustain her newfound lifestyle, or would it? This is the true reason of why she did it. It was not so she could just be with her friends and her grandchildren, it was for the satisfaction of her needs. Just as Maslow said many years ago, there is the satisfaction of needs that must be met. For Mercedes, that fateful night that destroyed my entire family (or at least the family that I have known for the past 25 years) those needs were jealousy and greed!

Slowly but surely during 2016 my financial picture started to improve. Sometime near mid-summer I was sitting on my back lanai when one of the yard men that was cutting my grass knocked on my screen enclosure door. This was highly unusual, but at the same time I had a deep conviction that this individual was actually sent to me. Something similar to "knock and the door shall open." The gentleman came up and introduced himself as Jesse. I offered him a glass of ice water. He thanked me for the ice water and drank it readily down. Then he told me why he stopped by. He said, "The Lord told me to come and talk with you" or words to this effect. He asked if I was a believer in Christ and I said yes and that I was trying to improve on my belief. He asked me if he could pray for me, in which case I readily accepted. Jesse became a regular visitor, stopping by at least once every week for several weeks. Each time I would get him a glass of ice water and we would talk. He eventually invited me to his church which was over in Winter Haven. He told me that they did a group meeting every Tuesday and Thursday evening and asked if I would go. I accepted his invitation, and I went to his church. When I arrived, I was suspicious because the church was not actually where he told me it was and I had to meet up with his wife, a woman that I had no connection with at all, and drive to another location. When I arrived at this new location it was in the parking lot of a very large and substantial church. I was told, however, not to park in the church parking lot but over on the edge of the grass. When I asked why, I was told something along the lines that the larger church disapproved of Jesse's church utilizing their parking lot during the week. I then realized that his ministry was a ministry for the homeless. Feeling rather guilty that I was eating their food, I asked the preacher how he was able to pay for all this. He told me that he received donations from here and there and then he asked if he could pray for me. Of course, I told him yes and I also gave him $20 to help support his ministry. He prayed for me to be healed and placed his hands upon me. I remember that his hands were very warm. Of course, an individual who is a doubter may wish this to be an instant healing, and then be left disappointed when this "healing" did not occur. I tried not to have this feeling, but I stayed after dinner to attend their service. This service was in a structure that could be equated to a double wide trailer which was situated on the edge of the parking lot facing a busy road. The structure had a ramp to accommodate my power chair, so I was able to have access. During the service, the preacher used my story as an illustration to the others. I did not mind but I felt somewhat shy because I considered that most individuals present did not have merely one 10th of what I had accumulated. The preacher then went on and selected a woman that was in her mid-40s, by my judgment, and asked her if she wanted to be filled with the joy of the Holy Ghost. She, of course, said yes or words to that effect. The preacher then laid hands on her and she almost instantly fell face first onto the ground laughing hysterically! For the next 45 minutes or so, by my recollection, she incurred moments of hysterical outbursts while the preacher continued to deliver his message. This all occurred across the room from where I was sitting and my last vision of Jesse was him kneeling over the woman, who was still laying on the ground laughing hysterically, putting his hand on her back and then looking straight at me. His eyes locked on to my eyes and I could tell he wanted to know if I believed what I was seeing. It was as if he was in my head. Mind you, no words were exchanged but I remember the question being presented in my mind and I just said no. I guess I did not pass the test for I've never seen Jesse again. I tried to contact the church because I was actually interested in buying them small Bibles to hand out during their service, but I was unsuccessful in this attempt. Several months later I asked my caregiver who drove me over to Winter Haven, if he still had Jesse's phone number in his phone. I asked this caregiver to contact Jesse. About two or three weeks went by and the caregiver finally received a text back just saying that his (Jesse's) route had been changed and he would no longer be servicing my account. In retrospect, my only explanation for these events is that Jesse was an Angel sent here to test my level of faith and I failed the test.

Sometime later, and I am speaking several months later, I received another potential visitation. I had a caregiver that was new on my account, asked me if she could come 30 minutes before her shift to answer any question that I may have about the Bible. I told her that she was certainly welcome to do so but presently I did not have any real questions. I was, however, having various caregivers read the Bible to me during their individual shifts. After she left, I thought it was interesting that she would just assume that I had questions or even feel comfortable enough to ask me anything at all about the Bible. For several weeks she would come by and talk to me about numerous things in including how to handle feelings that I would have from time to time. She told me that whenever I started thinking about these past events with Mercedes, her family, or the literal destruction of my family, that these were ploys from the Devil. She asked me if I started to have these types of thoughts, did I get depressed. I, of course said that I did. She told me that in order to prevent this level of depression from setting in, I needed to say almost as a mantra, "I rebuke you in the name of Jesus Christ." She told me to say this over and over until the feeling passed. She told me this was the devil's way of making me feel sad because that is the way he (Satan) wanted me to feel. She said something to the effect that as a father don't you want your children to feel good? To this of course I responded of course I did or something to this effect. She said "exactly. That is the way Our Father wants us to feel." It is only Satan that wants us to feel bad. I have used this technique on numerous occasions, and I can tell you that it truly does work! She still stops by to see me from time to time and has encouraged me to accept a baptism. I was baptized when I was a baby by my grandfather, who was also a minister. I felt that if his baptism was not any good, then I did not want any other. However, the more I contemplated this, the more I actually desired to carry this out and be baptized once again.

Almost every time I tried to arrange for my baptism, I met another obstacle in getting a baptism and be truly born again. At first it was how to clamp off my nose so that when I was dipped under the water it would not race into my nose. This was soon resolved."

"And how is that" questioned Catherine.

"While I was at the VA" John explained, "on one of many appointments, I had a breathing treatment from a pulmonologist in which they used a disposable clamp that would fit my purposes. Retaining it, I thought to myself, step one accomplished! My next step was to purchase decent clothing suitable for a baptism. Walmart proved to be most accommodating in this regard. Step two, accomplished. The next step that I was confronted with was trying to find the sling for my pool lift which had not been used for over a year. To explain matters further, I have a lift that is capable of picking me up out of my power chair and placing me into my Jacuzzi. It has a special sling with a set of chains that are used to accomplish this task. The search for the sling did not prove to be nearly as problematic as the search for the chains that lifted the sling up in order to place me into the Jacuzzi turned out to be. These chains had always hung from the pool lift on the back porch. After one of my sons (Daniel) parties with some of his friends, I went outside, and I noticed that my chains were missing. He (Daniel) who now in his adult life seems to be anti-religious, said he put the chains up for safekeeping. One thing led to another and through his own procrastination, I allowed him to leave for Iraq approximately six months later without recovering my chains. At any rate, I had ordered chains online which cost me up to $250."

"So, did you carrying out? Are you, born again" asked Catherine inquisitively.

"Why yes, yes, I am! It was the best thing I ever did" John said rather triumphantly. "You see I introduced to a pastor who is from a small Hispanic church. He came over to my house with several other parishioners and baptized me in my Jacuzzi the day before Easter 2017."

"Amazing" Catherine exclaimed. "I mean to say someone who's gone through all this, and you seem so calm, it is unbelievable, just unbelievable!"

"The level of grace and the level of peace that I have received from my Lord is just that, unbelievable" John said quite contentedly. "In an attempt to make sense out of what happened to my wife, that I worshiped and adored (perhaps this was the problem) or that I would do anything for, how could she do this? What would drive her to such an end? I have these questions and I asked God, quite some time ago, to please help me understand how this could've happened. Several months later I received my answer in almost a vision. It was two things, yes just two things. But these two things are often the biggest sins of all. It was jealousy and greed, or greed and jealousy have it any way you wish; like Burger King."

"And of your wife" questioned Catherine. "Whatever happened to her? I hope she got life."

"Ah good old Florida justice system" John said with a smile. "Remember I said waiting tell my sons about this was my downfall" John questioned. "Well, it seems like after she had served 300 days in jail she was released on house arrest. She remained on house arrest for just about one year. During this whole time, I had been praying. I prayed for her salvation, as I still do, and I even prayed for her boyfriend. This was a very hard thing for me to do, but I knew I had to."

"And why did you feel this way" Catherine asked.

"The Bible teaches us that we must pray for all sinners" John responded resolutely. "During this time, I remember praying that I did not want to see her go to jail for the rest of her life, but I did want a conviction. Now you may find me strange on this," then John paused for a moment to gather his thoughts

"Not at all" said Catherine and motioned for John to continue.

"You see as a Christian it is not unusual to have open communication with the Holy Spirit. After praying about the subject for so long, the Holy Spirit guided me towards grace."

"Grace" exclaimed Catherine. "This would be the last thing on my mind."

"Exactly" interjected John. "Mind you that originally this was the furthest thing on my mind! I mean originally my friends and I joked about getting T-shirts printed up with the name of the boat on it and sit in the front row during sentencing."

"Why" questioned Catherine. "What was the name of the boat?"

"*Living the dream*" John responded. "That was the name of the boat. Probably would've made a pretty good image as somebody got dragged off to jail. But that would've been considered too prideful. But rather Grace was how I was led. In reminding back on the part of the Bible that talks about *Judge not least ye be judged*, rang in my ears. You see, from what I have begun to understand is that Grace is what you receive when you deserve a much stricter level of punishment. This is what Jesus taught on Calvary. Grace, or at least the concept of it guided me towards accepting any outcome that would find her guilty. So, when the district attorney wanted to offer her a plea deal, I did not object."

"What sort of plea deal" asked Catherine.

"That the charge of attempted murder be dropped but she would have to plead guilty to the lesser charge of cruelty to the handicap. I thought this might be a fitting charge because she often talked about when she was a young girl there was a handicap child that she had to ride with on the bus to school. Mercedes would talk about how this child had to wear heavy metal braces on her legs, possibly due to polio, but

I am unsure. This child apparently would hit people with these heavy braces and laugh about it. Mercedes would talk about this often and say something to the effect that this was why she did not like handicap people. So being found guilty of cruelty to the handicap just seemed rather fitting."

"I would say so" said Catherine as she made more annotations on her notepad. "I mean if somebody trying to kill me, I don't think I be so magnanimous. But that's just me."

"Oh, trust me" said John reassuringly "the Holy Spirit dragged me to this acceptance rather kicking and screaming" John explained. "At the same time when I die and am pulled up to be judged, I certainly want to be handled with a certain level of Grace, so I consented. But that is not the real rub! There is actually a much *tougher pill to swallow.*"

"I can't imagine what that would be," said Catherine. "It seems like you already had quite a few *tough pills.*"

"Florida, for divorce, is a no-fault, community property state" John said.

"What's that supposed to mean" inquired Catherine.

"What that means is in Florida no matter what the other one did, marital assets are to be divided 50-50. This meant that even though she tried to kill me she was entitled to 50% of my retirement."

"What" exclaimed Catherine! "That is outrageous! I can't believe that."

"Neither could I" explained John. "But I have had at least four attorneys confirm this with me. Let me tell you I was absolutely livid! But once again, I prayed. I prayed long and hard and eventually what she received out of the divorce was less than 10% of my monthly income. And what made it even better is that it was recorded as alimony which she has to pay taxes on, and I get to deduct."

"Unbelievable" Catherine said that she just sat there shaking her head. "So, in the end, she gets rewarded" questioned Catherine.

"I'm not sure I would call it a reward" said John as he took another sip of water. "Money is just materialistic. The real reward awaits us all."

Catherine just sat there astonished by what she heard. Not only was she flabbergasted by the tale that she just heard, then the lack of any form of social justice would be enough to tip the scales of sanity in most people. But that's not what she was finding. Instead, the person before her had an incredibly calm spirit. "How can you sit there and not be bothered by this" questioned Catherine.

"Oh, trust me" John said reassuringly "it was difficult in the beginning. But as the good Lord said in the beginning "it will be okay."

CHAPTER THREE

. . .the bitter end

"So let me just tell you what I have learned from all of this" John began. He then very methodically begins to explain many things to Catherine. There are many things she wanted to know and things she did not want to know. But he attempted to explain. So as a good therapist she just let him deliver what would equate to yet another soliloquy.

"The great I Am that manifested Himself before Moses is just as alive today as He was 2000 years ago and as He was 5000 years ago! The God of Abraham, of Jacob, of David is just as alive and active today as He ever has been. This is just not something that happened 2000 years ago. God is real and that God is just as active today in our society and He was long ago. This is not something that can be rebuked by the so-called *Big Bang Theory* which seems to be so popular today. This is real! If nothing else, I want my story to stand in testament of that! I have been and still am a sinner. Probably one of the bigger ones that I have ever known. Yet God forgave me. My sin had me dead to rights, as is often said. I was weighed down and yet I did not know it. There was an evil cloud over me and over everything I own. It was present in my house. It was present in my thoughts. What I mean by this is I cannot stop thinking about the events that occurred. I couldn't believe all the evil and the deceit that I uncovered. I mean" and John' voice changed, and a veil of vulnerability seemed to move over him. "What I mean is the individual that I cherished above all others, that I trusted with truly my very life betrayed me so bitterly. That image is very hard to shake. Night after night I only sleep maybe one or two hours. Invariably almost every night I wake up right around 3 o'clock in the morning. This is especially true if I am in unfamiliar surroundings, such as a hospital. The only way I've made it through all of this is because of God! Laying in my bed at night with thoughts swirling in my head, on numerous occasions these thoughts have brought me close to the verge of quite possibly a breakdown. On several occasions I just felt and over whelming heavy weight of sadness, remorse, and utter loneliness. The only way I was able to sleep was through prayer."

"I don't mean to interject, well yes, I do mean to interject" insisted Catherine. "I see many patients, some much worse off than you, if you can believe that. I see patients with extreme PTSD, drug addictions, medical conditions that render them more vulnerable than you and I don't see where prayer would help them. So are you trying to tell me that all your problems just magically drifted or melted away" Catherine said with a certain tone that only signaled disbelief.

"I know you don't believe" said John again looking at his hands. "You're like so many others. There so many other people that I've talked to about this, to include supposedly church people and I get the same reaction. There was one church leader that I mentioned this to, and he acted almost jealous, but I'm telling you it's true, all the way down to the last syllable. Once I became saved, I mean born again, I see things differently. What used to interest me no longer does."

"Like what" questioned Catherine.

"Many things" said John in an attempt to clarify. "Things like drinking alcohol, cursing, pornography, or even listening to classic rock I no longer even have an interest in" explained John. "When I became saved, I prayed for our Lord Jesus Christ to take my problems, to take my fears, and take my anxiety and do with them as he will. I said Lord, I leave these at your feet do with them as you will. Ever since then my life has been at peace. I don't mean that I live just a casual, ho-hum life. What I mean is there is an inner peace inside of me that is so calming and beautiful that I cannot imagine being without it. Our Lord Jesus Christ gave me peace through all of this. Our Lord also gave an understanding."

"An understanding" questioned Catherine. "I mean I grew up as a good Catholic girl, so I think I have a fairly good idea and understanding of the Bible, but I don't have an inner peace."

"This is why you must be born again. According to the book of John, no one can get to heaven unless through Jesus Christ. This is why the act of being born again is so important." John said emphatically. "I didn't believe this either, but I do now. In trying to understand what happened in my life," John said and then took a long sip of water from his straw. He then leaned his head back, the best he could given the restraints of his headrest and looked up while holding his eyes closed. He held this position for just a moment before he began again. "It has often been said that Satan cannot directly affect mankind. Satan must choose other methods in order to affect mankind. This is because Satan lacks the energy force from God necessary to affect us.

As it tells us in the book of Job, for Satan to intervene with mankind must come by permission from God or if mankind opens the door to sin. As with my case I'm not sure if the door was opened in 2004 when I went to the Swinger's party or if there was always something inside of her possibly passed on from her father."

"*Interesting deflection*" Catherine thought to herself. "*I wonder why his thinking is this way, possibly deflecting some form of guilt or level of inadequacy on himself*" Catherine thought to herself.

Unbeknownst to John of these thoughts, he continued "one must remember that Satan is a legalist. He watches everything you do or say, looking for an opportunity to intervene in mankind."

"You say this as if you believe it and as if there is a war going on around us for our very souls" Catherine said while waving her hands in the air in disbelief.

"You see" John said. "It's that same level of disbelief that you just displayed that keeps you from accepting what I'm trying to say. I find it amazing that people are so willing and ready to accept the fact that there is evil in the world. You see it in movies, television shows or in everyday life. We are to ready and willing to accept this as a form of reality yet when it comes to accepting our Lord Jesus Christ, this is the reaction that most people give, all the while claiming that they are of Christian background."

"But you have to admit that this rather difficult to believe" Catherine insisted.

"Why?" For now, it was John' turn to ask questions. "It is that level of disbelief that Satan has sowed that prevents us from understanding. You see" John explained, there is a war going on, call it a war for our very souls. In order for us to better understand, God sent out a series of rules (call them laws) for mankind not to do. If mankind does not do certain things, Satan does not have the ability to intervene. It's when mankind does things like Eve eating the apple as it states in Genesis. She was told not to do this yet when she did it, the action itself opened the door for Satan to enter and make her aware things, like the fact that she did not have clothing on as an example, again, as it is written in Genesis.

Let's look at this a different way, Christians always talk about God the Father, in which case He truly is. Each of us are also brothers and sisters in Christ. For those of us who have been blessed to have children we know that if children are left alone, they are bound to get into something or do something that we, as parents, disapprove of. We all know that a child needs discipline and to be taught right from wrong. Children, when they're born, are brought into this world with a penchant for doing wrong. What I mean by this is no one had to teach a child how to not tell the truth. No one had to teach a child how to be greedy or how to desire something that is not theirs. These are all traits that we are "born" with. A parent who does not discipline their child or take the time to teach their child right and wrong are doing that child a disservice. The same holds true for God the Father.

In the beginning God gave us all free will. There are those who would argue that this was God's greatest gift to mankind while others will argue this was our ultimate downfall. Initially of course God looked to punish Adam and Eve for disobeying His command of not eating the forbidden fruit. This punishment, was the banning of Adam and Eve from the Garden of Eden, sentencing man let out a life of "sweat from the brow again as it is written in Genesis 3: 23 and Eve, as well as the rest of womankind to have pain during childbirth, again, I quote from Genesis 3: 16. Some time went on then God saw how evil and corrupt mankind actually became so God set out to destroy the entire world.

Later on, as mankind continued to veer off course, God set out to destroy, what He viewed as the center of this evil, being Solomon and Gomorrah. Again, this can be found in Genesis 18: 20.

It was at this point that as our spiritual father, God set out to teach us the proper way that He wishes for us to live and worship Him, and He alone. After establishing "The Law" which was given to Moses and establishing the order of how mankind was to worship God. This is all laid out in 1 Thessalonians 2:13. However, God knew our hearts and our penchant for doing those things that we are not supposed to do. Therefore, God established, through a series of sacrifices of unblemished animals (such as lambs, goats, cattle etc.), a method by which mankind could seek forgiveness and atonement for those times that we stray from the true path that He laid out before us. We as parents do something very similar whenever our child disobeys. We do not turn to our child with an unforgiving heart. Neither does our Father.

In the grand scheme of things, prior to the establishment of The Law, sin was not really identified. By this I mean in The Law mankind was told what to do and what not to do. Hence, anything that was against The Law was thereby a sin. So, The Law established what was right and wrong. It was even after this that mankind continues to sin regardless of receiving the law and years of providing sacrifices to God to atone for our behavior. It was at this point that God sent his only son, our Lord Jesus Christ. As Jesus ascended to heaven, he gave mankind the gift of the Holy Spirit as explained in the book of Matthew chapter 28, verses 18–20, I believe.

The Holy Spirit originates in God, flows through Jesus to affect mankind. According to the works by the biblical scholar Erickson in 2000, the Holy Spirit, for the lack of a better term, is an energy source that allows for free communication between God, Jesus and mankind. Considering it is this a force that flows from God through Jesus and into mankind (and vice versa) it is not privy to Satan. To obtain access to this wonderful gift, one must first ask for God the Father to open one's heart and soul for acceptance to the Holy Spirit. Once the Holy Spirit is within you, you become "marked" as a Christian and this is often manifested by being baptized in the Holy Spirit in which one will respond in a method that is often referred to as speaking in tongues. Once having the Holy Spirit within you, the Holy Spirit can be called upon to talk with you on a regular basis. This way you can have an open and running conversation within the Trinity which can provide you with daily guidance on all aspects of life. One might ask why it is set up this way where mankind must ask for the Holy Spirit to enter their soul and heart. This is because God gave mankind the element of "free will." As such, we must choose to follow God's law that God gave to Moses carved in stone. Without God's law, there is no sin. Everything therefore is connected in which without good there is no evil. Without daylight there is no darkness. The concept of separating the two become so blurred that one cannot differentiate between the two.

Many of these things are not explained initially. It's a learning process just like life itself. Whenever you have a child, or even a pet, discipline becomes a major factor in how a child or pet is going to act and behave. Without an element of discipline and/or rules of proper behavior, the child or pet is not received well in society. These rules of proper behavior are often established as social norms. For a child it would be something simple like asking permission before they do something or by saying yes ma'am and no ma'am. For a pet it could be simply being housebroken. Whatever it is in societal norms. It is the rules of behavior that have been established as something that is considered "acceptable." At the same time, when your child asks you "why" they must do certain things or behave a certain way you may or may not find it necessary or even "proper" at the time to explain your reasoning's. The same thing goes for God. God is our Father. If I am a child of God so is the rest of mankind. This is where the element of "free will" comes into play. It is "free will" which allows us to accept the fact of this father-child relationship or not. If we accept it, then we must live by the elements of what is considered acceptable societal norms which means those items that are carved in stone and provided to Moses. One of the most essential of these "laws" is the very first one in which we are not have any other gods before God. This was part of my downfall in that I do believe I placed my wife, Mercedes, on a "pedestal" which in effect placed her before God. A good number of times modern man gets too wrapped up with the "here and now" to fully understand this. I am just as guilty as everyone else, and I still don't think I have this correct. This is all a very much a work in progress but so is life itself.

My failures in life, I believe, have all been due to the fact that I have broken this very first law in that I have placed other things in my life to be more important than God himself. The first thing I have placed as being more important was always money or the lack thereof or the need, therefore. I have worked sometimes 18+ hours a day in order to provide what I felt was a comfortable income and way of life for my family. Never once during this time that I ever took the time out to even speak to God let alone going to church on Sunday. Sunday was always a day to watch football and grade school papers while sitting in my easy chair. If I was not doing this, I was usually out in the yard working or floating in my pool drinking a cocktail. Never once did I ever place God first in my life.

As long as you have God in your life, and placed first, it is very difficult, but not impossible, for Satan to affect you."

"If you do all these things" Catherine asked "how is it possible that Satan can still affect you" Catherine asked inquisitively. *It was at this point that Catherine's interest was aroused.*

Sensing this, John continued, "you see according to Bradley, yet another biblical scholar, in an undated publication, for Satan to affect someone, one must first open "a door" which could be allowing certain individuals or certain items into your home, drugs and alcohol, indulging in pornography, watching questionable movies that are based upon the occult, or are demonic. This, I believe is at the "root" of my current state of affairs. It was not just the aforementioned, but rather it was and remains to be *pleasures of the flesh.* Just as Moses and Aaron were denied access to the promised land as it tells us in the book of Numbers, because of my womanizing ways and the associated loose interpretations of "marriage," I purposely ruined two families simply to satisfy my desires. As a consequence, for this lifestyle or "lie choices" I too have been denied that basic pleasure people receive in their old age, the right to play with their grandchildren. It is because of my earlier choices that I now sit here motionless as a matter of atonement. Other behaviors could be things such as going to mediums and have your fortune read or even playing with the Ouija board. Satan and Demons are always present, and they even use family members or even church members in order to potentially corrupt an individual. The basic message here is one must always be on guard for such attempts because it is actually an ongoing war between good and evil in which we are the pawns.

It has taken me quite some time quite a few hours of prayer to come to understand that my ex-wife, who I still dearly love, was consumed by the Jezebel spirit. I'm not sure how long she had spirit or exactly how she contracted it, but I know that she was under the Jezebel spirit's influence."

"Jezebel" I've heard of this Catherine remarked. "Isn't this supposed to be some type of voluptuous woman that steals the hearts of men" questioned Catherine.

"Something like that" responded John. "Although not mentioned directly, and mind you I'm not a biblical scholar but the first real mention of such a woman, that I can find, is in Proverbs 5 and then again in Isaiah 47:7-9. In this text she is described as a lover of pleasure. Further readings I have had on the subject I have found that someone who is of the Jezebel spirit is an individual that craves pleasure of the flesh."

"Isn't that most men" Catherine asked with a small smile.

"Well, I assume so" John responded, "but this is different. Men, I believe, are more wrapped with pleasure it brings."

"So, why do you believe that is so different for women" Catherine asked inquisitively.

"Well," John began, "when I first met her, she was so interested in having sex, numerous times a day that I used to refer to her as a nymphomaniac. Which, of course, is just about every man's dream! But this went further than that and it didn't really come out until after we were married. Now, mind you when I'm about ready to say is information that I have derived from several different scholars. There are some variations, of course, depending on who you read but there seems to be a consensus on certain traits."

"Traits" Catherine asked. This time she actually put her pencil down and looked like she was interested in the topic of discussion.

"Yes, traits, common characteristics of individuals that are considered to be consumed with this form of spirit" John explained. "Now mind you this form of spirit is highly intelligent and is one of the most evil of all spirits commanded by the Dark One."

"And by the Dark One are you referring to Satan" questioned Catherine more for clarification than of interest.

"Why yes" responded John. "Under this form of a dark spirit, the female rather lures in her prey through the temptation of the male desire for pleasures of the flesh, or do you not believe in Satan's existence either or his ability to affect our lives?"

"Why I do believe that some people believe in this type of existence, but you have to admit these were tales from the past" Catherine responded with a smile. "You cannot possibly believe in these types of existence in this day of age."

John mood and demeanor took a sudden change to the seriousness, "do you mean to tell me that you are not a believer in good and evil?"

"Well as a therapist I can tell you that there is good and evil in everyone, and it does not take some supernatural being to bring it out" Catherine responded matter-of-factly.

John was truly agitated at this point "do you mean to tell me that you do not believe in life after death? Have I not yet convinced you, just through my discussion that there is a higher power?"

"As I told you in the beginning I was raised as a Catholic. In this regard yes, I do. It is just hearing it, in the clinical setting seems to be rather passé, so to speak" Catherine responded rather indignantly.

"Why do you find it so difficult to discuss issues of life and death" questioned John. "I think you're trying to spend time in studying me, but I think it's time to turn this around and explore why you have reasons not to believe." John then took another sip of water through his straw before continuing. "I mean this is serious stuff! I did not necessarily believe in this either until I was confronted with it! Now, I know it's real and I'm glad to be called a child of God."

Either sensing his frustration or addressing an issue that was too painful for her, Catherine pressed to redirect the line of questioning. "Tell me more of this Jezebel spirit."

"I shall, and through it I pray that it will bring about this belief in yourself" John responded with a smile. "As I stated, this particular spirit is a very intelligent spirit and is one of the evilest. In dealing with her, she never admits to being wrong. No matter what you do, and it does not matter if one truly knows better, everyone else is always wrong and she is always correct. Just like with the issue when she went to the hospital in a coma. She had evidently written a suicide note the night before, yet she claimed that I wrote the note."

"You wrote the note" questioned Catherine. "But you're a quadriplegic, unable to use your hands."

"My you catch on quick" smiled John. "There is another explanation offered and that was that I poisoned her. When I pointed out the fact that I could not stand up, it was suggested that I have been faking all these years."

Catherine adjusted slightly before asking the obvious "faking, faking what."

"She tried to claim that I was faking my illness and I could actually walk" John said with a smile. "When I pointed out that I have to be a really good faker, it was quickly brushed aside and then I was accused of having my 400-pound, 6 foot five friend sneak into the house and urinate in her bottle of rum. To further complicate things throughout these trials and tribulations, she tried to claim various things such as she was only attempting to adjust my pillow or that nothing of this sort happened and it was just me on drugs."

"Well just by taking what you at, say at face value, without any follow-up or cross examination of her, I can say that making outlandish statements such as what you are reporting does not make her some form of ancient biblical demon" Catherine said. "I know it's something you wish to believe, but it does not make it so."

"Oh, I realize that" John said as he adjusted his chair slightly. "There are other things, such as her constant lying, saying things such as the boat was her boyfriends or that she was a widow. She is also very quick to take credit for everything that is good. She would often say that the only reason why I had my job at the city was because of her and the way she looked. She would often say that the only reason why people looked at me favorably is because I could not possibly be a loser and be married to somebody as nice as she was. Whenever you attempted to confront her by using logic, she would just attempt to confuse the subject by entering in five or six different reasons or explanations, as to why the same issue that was at hand was not possibly the way you envisioned it, all the while covering up her true intent."

"Can you give me an example of this" offered Catherine as she was busily taking notes.

John thought for a minute and then offered "she was consumed with the withholding of information or distorting information to the extent that you would no longer want to ask the question or were so thoroughly confused that you lost interest in the subject and therefore you would no longer ask questions. Most notably along the lines would have to be explanations regarding her financial dealings. Whenever I would ask how things are going to be paid or how things were going to be accomplished, I would receive tremendous backlash and doubletalk to the extent that you would not want to press the subject. Further, she was the self-proclaimed absolute authority on all matters dealing with religion, religious thought or understanding what the Bible really had to say. This was so prevalent that when my boys came home from school with questions about the Bible, she would take over and offer her interpretation and get very upset if I suggested that we read the Bible together with them. This suggestion was almost instantly shot down with such argument that one would not wish to pursue the discussion any longer. I ended up reading the Bible to my sons in secret."

"In secret" questioned Catherine, as she scribbled quickly to catch up. "Dare I ask?"

"I had to not only hide the Bible, but I had to hide the fact that I was reading it."

"On another occasion I remember we were watching this religious movie and at the end of the movie the narrator mentioned that Moses was buried by *the hand of God.* One of my sons questioned how something like this could occur. For the next 30 minutes or so my son and his mother were engaged in a heated conversation about how something like that could occur. Now mind you my son, at the time, was in middle school. Yet this conversation went on to the extent that he stood up in an attempt to leave and she (Mercedes) chased after him. For safety purposes he ran into our walk-in pantry and barred the door. Almost every chance she got she would cut down individuals or individual churches as being foolish or crazy. I had always gone to church on Sundays. I was not the most religious person nor was I the most righteous, but I did go. Two of my bigger highlights of the year was always to go to Easter Sunrise service and Christmas Eve candlelight service."

"Again, many people love these services" Catherine interjected.

"True" nodded John in agreement. "But I would not believe that a rational, logical grown woman would go to the extent and claim that my going to an Easter Sunrise service with my two children from a previous marriage as grounds for joining the Swinger's club" John said with a certain level of agitation that clearly displayed not only disgust at the thought but also a certain air of bewilderment. "And don't even get me started about Christmas Eve."

"What was wrong with Christmas Eve" questioned Catherine.

"You name it! Everything was wrong. I really liked going to the one large church's in town yet she claimed that she could not go because of all of the hypocrites that were going there as well."

"How did she know they were hypocrites" asked Catherine.

"Her friends from high school were also members of that church. She tried to get reattached with them, but they rather gave her the cold shoulder. Therefore, they instantly became hypocrites although she had not had anything to do with them in close to 40 years."

"Are these the same people that she expressed jealousy over" questioned Catherine again in an attempt to clarify the earlier statement and to find some form of linkage back to what was said earlier.

"Yes, these are the same people" John said before continuing on. "There were other instances that she would throw out as to why we could not go for Christmas candlelight service. She would throw these elaborate parties on Christmas Eve yet only invite her family and no one else. Even if the Christmas Eve service were to be held later in the evening, after her party to be over, she would refuse to go. It got to be such a fight that it took the entire spirit of the evening and turn it into a major kerfuffle which just served to ruin the mood.

There were other occasions, not just these two particular events. I remember one Christmas Eve where we had five children involved in the live nativity scene."

"Oh, I always like to see those" Catherine interjected.

"Yes, they are nice to see. They rather bring out the sanctity of the season" John said in agreement. "Although I do agree that there should be some form of celebration when you consider the moment that such a live nativity scene is representing, celebration is not what people come to see."

Curious as to what he said Catherine interrupted once again by asking, "What do you mean."

"What I mean by this" John offered in clarification "people do not come to view a live nativity scene only to watch some middle school girl jumping up and down and flaring her arms everywhere."

"Who did this" questioned Catherine.

"Her daughter, my stepdaughter" John said with an air of disgust.

"Is this Tammy? Well, what happened" questioned Catherine as she attempted to draw out more information.

"Yes, this was Tammy. I can also tell you that I was livid! All the other children that participated did so in a solemn and reverent manner, as one would expect, and proper behavior would dictate. But, oh no, our child was the one acting up, so much so she was asked to leave."

"Who asked her" Catherine asked again inquisitively.

"There was someone there from the church that was trying to supervise and control the children that were involved. So of course, when Tammy was asked to leave, we had to take all our four children out which destroyed the entire event."

"But I digress," said John. "I was saved two other times by the Holy Spirit so I know that he has a special purpose for me."

"Oh," asked Catherine inquisitively. "In which two times were these?"

"In 2018 I had a caregiver come to the house that you did tell was physically sick."

Catherine finished writing a few notes and then asked, "what you mean?"

"You can tell just by looking at her. Her eyes were swollen, she had a runny nose, and was coughing."

"Then why did you let her in" asked Catherine rather pointedly. "If it were me, it stands to reason that I went her in just on that basis alone."

"Yes," John said, and again looking at his useless hands. "I let her in simply because she was a single parent with four children to support. The problem was not so much in the fact that she was sick, but the fact that she did not abide by mask discipline rules."

Again, Catherine interrupted, "and how is that?"

"Every time I looked at her," John explained, "her mask would be down below her nose. Now, ordinarily this may not be such a big problem. But, for me, the problem was she was brushing my teeth and I was just sitting there with my mouth wide open, with her breathing right down on me. Within a week, I had become deathly ill with influenza B, pneumonia, and yet another urinary tract infection. Now I realize that she did not give me the last one, but I certainly know I got the influenza

B from her, and this is what would put me over the edge. I was so sick, and I remember the EMTs saying they didn't know they have enough time to get from my house to the main hospital in town which was a level II trauma center. However, I got to this hospital and remain there for quite some time."

"How long were you there" question Catherine. In doing so, she flipped through her notes to see if there is any indication of this illness. "Your notes here do not indicate any such stay. Did you at any time reach out to the VA for assistance during this time?"

"No ma'am, I wanted to live not just sit in the ER unattended for three or four hours, like I have in the past whenever I've come to the VA emergency room. And, oh by the way, the VA is about an hour away, on a good day" explained John. "But, once again I digress. While I was in the hospital, I was so ill that at one point I was almost coded out, meaning they were about ready to pronounce me dead. This was only after a series of attempts to get me to wake up and breathe normally. At one time, my caregiver tells me that a nurse was standing at the head of my bed leaning over my body, giving the chest compressions but to no avail. It was only after they put a mask over my face with the intent of forcing air into be by compressing a very large balloon type bag that was attached to the mask. After only one compression, I immediately woke up! This, naturally, surprised the ER staff, to the point that the doctor asked me how I did this. Of course, I said I don't know, or words to that effect."

"Well, you must admit that would've been very dramatic and not something that occurs on a regular basis."

"True," said John prior to taking the other on water on his long straw. "For the rest of the time in the hospital, in the early morning twilight, when I was barely awake, you know, that period of half-awake and half-asleep, I remember faintly seeing the fluorescent lighting above. In that limited light I remember seeing little red dots flowing up from me to the light, and little green dots flowing down from the light to me. Now mind you, when I first saw this, I didn't realize what I was looking at. I thought it was some phenomenon of the bright lights shining in my barely awake eyes. But the more I came to realize it, it was the Holy Spirit intervening in my life and helping to cleanse my body of the illness.

Before I knew it, I was released from the hospital and sent home, straight from the ICU."

Again, Catherine was busy scribbling away on her notepad when she stopped and looked up and said, "what you have to admit that that was rather amazing. So," Catherine asked. "Was this your second time that you claim God saved you?"

"Why yes, yes it was" nodded John. "Now let me to you about the third time."

"That's right," Catherine agreed that she quickly flipped through her notes. "I do remember you mentioning something about that."

"Yes, I would agree," John admitted willingly. "But it was after they sent me home, that within 24-hour period I still did not feel any better, as a matter fact I was feeling worse. It got so bad that my caregiver had to call the ambulance once again. This time he took me to a smaller community hospital that I go to more often than not because I believe I get better care and I certainly get better food. This time, however, community hospital did not waste time and sent me to a more advanced hospital within their community of network of other hospitals. During all of this it would appear as if the medication I received at the trauma level II hospital created a bleeding ulcer in my pancreas! So that was my internal bleeding that I ended up taking five units of blood! I ended up having a team of doctors around me all trying to figure out what to do to stop the bleeding. I must've been there for several weeks. Finally, I asked my caregiver to contact my Hispanic preacher. It was a Sunday, I didn't really understand it was a Sunday because you, lose track of time when in the hospital. At any rate, after Sunday service he jumped in his car and drove at least an hour and ½ just to get to me. When he arrived, after a short visit, he laid hands on my stomach and prayed most of it was in Spanish, so I didn't really understand what he was saying. Later that night I felt a slight quivering in my stomach I knew what it was it was God!

Catherine just at back in amazement. After reading through her nose quickly, she looked up and asked "so you were saved three times."

"Yes, I can say emphatically yes! Although I have lived such a wretched life up until this point, had committed murder, was an adulterer and not just once but numerous times over, God still saw will it fit to save me" exclaimed John. "Even though I had repeatedly violated almost every one of the 10 Commandments, I still found it within His Grace to save the center such as I."

"So, what you're saying is" again interrupted Catherine, "if you can be saved, that almost anybody can be."

"You're absolutely correct" explained John. "One must first humble themselves before the Lord and earnestly beg for forgiveness and will be granted, no matter how bad of a sinner you are or were. The blood that was shed at Calvary, was meant for all of us" John explained.

Catherine sat there for a moment, then she very carefully placed her pencil inside of her note pad as a way of marking her spot. "So, you now claim that you are at peace."

"I do still claim," said John rather indignantly. "You will receive Grace. But, this relationship is not just a one-time deal" explained John. "This is a relationship like most relationships you have to work on it."

"And how does one do that" question Catherine with a rather judgmental tone.

"How does anybody work on many relationship" questioned John. "You work on it by staying in communications with your Lord and Savior. This is done through prayer. This is not a one-time deal. You should try to pray at least once or twice a day. If nothing else, God would like to just to hear from you, as any parent would. Sometimes you can pray and just let God know how you feel. I myself try to start off and thank him for everything that he has done for me."

"So," Catherine began, "where does all this leave everyone else?"

"Well, I have a permanent restraining order against Mercedes, so I have no contact with her, nor do I wish to. I'm sure wherever she is she is living off of somebody else's dime. David got another girl pregnant the same week as he got his wife pregnant."

"*Sounds like a chip off the old block*" that Catherine herself. "Please continue."

John took another long drink from a straw before continuing. "So now David has two boys, but neither one is allowed to have anything to do with."

"What you mean by that" question Catherine.

"Well, it seems like David has gotten remarried once again, but his new wife will not let him have anything to do with me or his mother because supposedly we have visitations with one of his sons. The other son, who was born out of wedlock, is the son of a religious young lady, who took a walk on the wild side, so to speak, when she picked up relations with him. At any rate, she is married, and her husband has taken to this little boy almost instantaneously! I could not ask for anything better."

"And your other son" question Catherine as she was flipping through her notes quickly find his name.

"You mean Daniel," questioned John. "He is doing great! We talked almost every day. He is actually now a Captain in the Army Reserve and has spent two tours overseas. One of those two words was in Syria and the other one was Kuwait. As a matter fact he just got back from serving in Kuwait. He is living up to West Virginia and the soon to be married to a very nice young lady from West Virginia. He, in speaking with him, could not be happier."

Catherine looked through her notes quickly, for she knew her time was just about up for this session. "So how are you doing?"

"Me," questioned John rather rhetorically. "I'm doing great! I'm a 100% peace, I get to give back two hours of my time twice a week in helping elementary school kids with their homework, support a food bank and Tithe on a regular basis. This is another important issue that as a Christian, that one must come to understand. God always gets the first 10% of anything that you do or earn."

"You mean you must give this money to the church" questioned Catherine.

"You not necessarily getting into the church," John responded. "You're giving it to support the ministry and help spread the word of the gospel. This," John said very emphatically, "is a must."

"Well, we've covered quite a bit and I can definitely say that what you're telling me about God and his acceptance of this really seems to be quite compelling" stated Catherine after she finished once again scribbling in her notepad. "You make it sound like anybody can do this."

"Anybody can" exclaimed John. "As I said, one must humble themselves before the Lord and earnestly ask for forgiveness, and it will be granted. The best way I think I can explain this all can be rather summed up it's something I learned growing up in the church."

"And what is this" question Catherine.

"It's something that's called the Apostle's Creed," explained John.

"I think I remember something like that when I was in Catholic school" Catherine said. "D you know how it goes?"

"Of course," responded John. "To the best of my recollection it goes; I believe in God the father Almighty maker of heaven and earth, and in Jesus Christ his only son our Lord who was conceived by the Holy Spirit born of the Virgin Mary, suffered under Pontius Pilate, was crucified dead and buried. On the third day he rose from the dead and sit with the right hand of God the father Almighty. From there He shall come to judge the quick and the dead. I believe in the holy catholic church, the communion of saints, the forgiveness of sins, and the life everlasting. Amen."

"With that," said Catharine, "I do believe our time is op" she said as she rose and once again extending out her hand ti offer a handshake goodbye. "*Stupid!*" Catherine thought to herself. "Sorry" was all she was able to say.

"Don't be" remarked John. "I find it rather amusing" John said with a smile. "It happens more often not." This John mentioned as he left her office.

www.ingramcontent.com/pod-product-compliance
Lightning Source LLC
Chambersburg PA
CBHW021004150626
46549CB00012BA/1058